Ethics for School Leaders

Setting Your Ethical Compass

Gary Hoban, PhD
Clifford Tyler, EdD
Barbara Salice, EdD

Kendall Hunt
publishing company

Kendall Hunt
p u b l i s h i n g   c o m p a n y

www.kendallhunt.com
Send all inquiries to:
4050 Westmark Drive
Dubuque, IA   52004-1840

Contents

Contents

Foreword

Writing a book about ethics in these times can be challenging. There can be little doubt that never a day goes by that one does not read of some ethical scandal somewhere. And that includes in the schools. That is why we decided to address the topic of ethics and school leadership and tie it to the development of one's personal ethical core, or as we call it, one's ethical compass.

This book, *Ethics for Today's School Leaders: Setting Your Ethical Compass,* has been written for those who are aspiring to become school leaders and are enrolled in an administrative preparation program which can lead to a state credential or certificate. It has also been written for everyone who has an interest in the subject and might want to think about how their school leaders are prepared and the kinds of materials they read and discuss.

The book is divided into seven chapters which introduce the subject of ethics, consider selected philosophical writings, examine leadership standards, explore ethics and diversity, ponder ethics and a woman's perspective, present case studies, and offer concluding thoughts. The book is the outgrowth of a course in ethics and school ethics taught at National University. Each of the three authors—Dr. Gary Hoban, Dr. Clifford Tyler, and Dr. Barbara Salice—has taught the course which was originally developed by Dr. Hoban. The authors are themselves seasoned veterans of work in public and private schools and have a number of years of experience teaching at the university level.

Dr. Gary Hoban has recently retired as a full-time faculty member at National University, a university initially designed to primarily serve the needs of adult, graduate-level students. For 21 years he has been a professor of educational administration and served as the founding chair of the Educational Administration Department, a position he occupied for many of those years. He has also served as the University's Dean of Graduate Studies, interim associate provost, and interim dean of the School of Education. Dr. Hoban has numerous publications from over the years, including work dealing with the concept of self-efficacy, online education, and school leadership. He has also presented at a number of national and international conferences. Prior to his work at National University, Dr. Hoban served for 25 years as a public school teacher and administrator in California, primarily as a curriculum supervisor, assistant superintendent for both instruction and personnel, and as an interim superintendent. He holds a PhD in Educational Administration from the University of California, Los Angeles, a Master of Arts in Teaching (English) from the University of Chicago, and a Bachelor of Arts from the University of Notre Dame.

Dr. Clifford Tyler has been a full-time faculty member at National University in the Department of Educational Administration for the past ten years, including 18 months as the Department Chair. While serving at National University, Dr. Tyler has made numerous presentations at both national and international conferences in Europe, the Middle East, Asia, Africa, and South America. He has written numerous professional journals and online articles on higher education/school district partnerships, online education, education leadership, and school district finance issues. Prior to his work at National University, Dr. Tyler served as both a district and county schools superintendent for 20 years in K–12 districts ranging in size from 200 students to 12,500 students in Oregon, Washington, California, and New Hampshire. He also served as headmaster of a private independent school for two years, has been both an elementary and high school principal for eight years, and a classroom teacher for six years, including the American School in Japan. Dr. Tyler holds an EdD from the

University of the Pacific in Educational Administration, an MEd from the University of Oregon in Elementary Education, and a Bachelor of Science degree from Oregon State University.

Dr. Barbara J. Salice holds a Doctorate in Education from the University of Southern California in the field of Higher, Adult and Professional Education. She has taught kindergarten through graduate school students. For five years she was involved in the creating and developing of literacy and basic skills programs for non-traditional students in the State of Hawaii. From 1996–1998, she served as Executive Director of the Literacy Network of Greater Los Angeles. Dr. Salice has had considerable experience in designing, directing, and implementing programs in leadership. She has trained faculty to teach online. Dr. Salice served as Vice-Chair of the Governor's Council for Literacy at its inception in 1990. She received Hawaii's First Lady's Volunteer of the Year Award in 1987 and is credited with operating the Outstanding Literacy Program for Hawaii for two years. She served as a chair of the Professional Development Committee of the Commission on Adult Basic Education for six years. Currently, she teaches online courses in Higher Education and Adult Learning for Walden University in the Doctorate of Education program and teaches as an adjunct professor at National University.

All three authors have collaborated on this book, but Dr. Hoban has focused on setting the direction for the text in the introduction, presenting and reflecting on philosophy and diversity, and co-authoring—with Dr. Tyler—the chapters that present case studies and the concluding thoughts. Dr. Tyler's primary focus, in addition to those chapters he shared with Dr. Hoban, has been on administrative standards and their application. Dr. Salice is the sole author of Chapter 5 on ethics and a woman's perspective, and she has chosen to present that chapter in the first person as it represents her personal and academic point of view on this often-controversial topic.

The authors wish to thank Joseph Wells, acquisitions editor for Kendall Hunt, without whose encouragement and support this book would not have been possible. We also wish to thank Lacey Reynolds, our manuscript coordinator at Kendall Hunt, for all of her assistance and Chelsea Beckham who worked with us earlier this year as we began our writing. Also, we wish to thank Dr. Ken Fawson, National University's Interim School of Education Dean, Dr. R. D. Nordgren, Chair of the Educational Administration Department, and our colleagues in that department at National University for their support and insight over the past year. And we especially want to acknowledge the insights and feedback provided by our students in the ethics and school leadership classes we have taught who are the true inspiration for this book.

Chapter 1

Why Do We Study Ethics?

Since 2001, major corporate scandals have seen executives imprisoned with the collapse of major corporations such as Enron, WorldCom, and Lehman Brothers, to name but a few. Enron executive Jeffrey Skilling went to jail and Enron Chairman Kenneth Lay died while awaiting trial. And one cannot forget the problems brought to the financial markets by Bernie Madoff, with many investors losing their retirement savings. Religious bodies, as well, have not been immune to ethical lapses with leading clergymen losing their posts. Two United States Catholic Cardinals retired from or left their archdioceses amid controversy regarding their handling of sexual abuse scandals, and ministers from other denominations have had to respond to the courts of law and public opinion because of alleged sexual improprieties. And so, too, some leaders of schools have been caught up in scandals as well.

Today, it is not uncommon for ethics to be a frequent topic of discussion. It is regularly cited as a concern in federal, state, and local government. The United States Congress has had its own ethical sense questioned by the electorate while struggling to set new standards of ethics for itself and others. At the federal level and elsewhere, it has been difficult to find consensus as to what is ethically appropriate and what is not.

Because of these scandals, especially in the business sector, an Internet search on the topic "ethics and education" yields countless entries regarding the offering of courses in business ethics. Many, if not most, business schools incorporate consideration of "business ethics" into their MBA programs, with many mandating a required course in the subject. A search for ethics courses in graduate educational leadership programs, however, does not provide the same results. While it would not be accurate to say there are none, there are, relatively speaking, only a few. Yet, educational leaders face many of the same challenges as leaders in other fields and equally—perhaps more so—need to bring a well-calibrated personal ethical compass to their work.

This brings us to the question we face as educators, especially those preparing to become school leaders—why should we study ethics? There are many who believe that educators, by their nature, begin their work as school leaders with a complete set of developed personal and professional ethics. In some instances, those who propose that aspiring school administrators formally study ethics are dismissed as out of touch professors who present just one more obstacle in the road to doing one's job. The study of ethics, these critics claim, is not rooted in the real world and is too much theory in a reality student-based environment.

The critics notwithstanding agree there is a real need to study ethics. Hardly a day goes by when one does not hear of some incident of a major ethical lapse in the judgment of those responsible for the education of children and young adults. In many cases these lapses may prove not to be matters of criminal legality, although they certainly can be. Whether or not they are legal matters, they are matters of compromised thought and action leading to unfortunate outcomes for students and to professional ruin for educators. While it not disputed that there are individuals who deliberately and knowingly act criminally and unethically, one can argue that most people do not deliberately want to act unethically. Somehow people, even school leaders, slide into questionable ethical behavior with significant consequences for not only themselves but also for those whom they serve. It is only when an ethical matter is in the past that those who have made wrong decisions ask themselves how they got themselves into the situation they find themselves in.

While we know that it is only recently that attention has been given to requiring the formal study of ethics in school leadership programs, general concern about ethical issues and the schools has been longstanding. One measure of that concern can be found in the number of entries one can find on the Internet through search engines such as Google. It is not unusual to find as many 50 million results—a staggering amount of news stories, articles, reflections, commentaries, questions, and inquiries regarding ethical issues and the schools as well as personal and institutional guides and policies for engaging in proper ethical behavior.

Perhaps no story regarding an ethical lapse captured the attention of the public like the story regarding the sexual abuse allegations at Pennsylvania State University in 2011. As shocking as the criminal charges against the former assistant football coach Jerry Sandusky were regarding the exploitation and sexual abuse of boys who participated in his Second Mile charity foundation, there were also the major ethical questions concerning the legendary football coach Joe Paterno and the president of the University, Graham Spanier. Both Paterno and Spanier lost their jobs because it was believed that they knew that there were reports of Sandusky's behavior over a period of years but they did not take sufficient action to prevent him from having continued access to children. It was observed at the time that Paterno and Spanier may have met the minimum legal requirements in the matter, but, in order to protect the reputation of the institution and its significance in intercollegiate sports, did not directly intervene and take action to prevent suspected ongoing abuse. In many ways they exercised benign neglect—a reasoned avoidance of a compelling moral issue in the name of a perceived greater good—of their own reputations and that of their institution.

Often, as suggested earlier, unethical behavior is not always illegal behavior. The law is quite specific about what is permissible and what is not. Ethical behavior, which, of course intersects with legal requirements in the majority of instances, also goes beyond the law and gets to the core of what most believe is right and appropriate behavior. In the Penn State case there were criminal statutes to be dealt with, but beyond that, there were matters of judgment that leaders such as Paterno and Spanier had to face. Overall, they had outstanding records of leadership in sports and higher education, but when the time came to make moral judgments that went beyond the law, in a time of crisis they were found wanting by many, including the Pennsylvania State University Board of Trustees. In an interview in mid-January 2012, Paterno observed, "I didn't know exactly how to handle it and I was afraid to do something that might jeopardize what the university procedure was, so I backed away and turned it over to some other people, people I thought would have a little more expertise than I did. It didn't work out that way." One can imagine both Paterno and Spanier asking themselves after the scandal broke, "What should I have done and when should I have done it?" There is no easy answer to those or like questions. In hindsight it appears that the answers are obvious, but they probably were not at the time. Nonetheless, as one becomes a leader in any field, there is an expectation that one has developed a personal set of ethics that parallels a professional set of ethics that allows for right decisions to be made at the right time.

In the public schools the ongoing pressure to raise student test scores in the 2000s created many ethical lapses by school administrators who thought they were doing the right thing in providing motivational impetus to teachers to raise scores—sometimes going so far as to cross the line into actual cheating that broke the law. In 2011, a major scandal in the Atlanta, Georgia public schools was reported in an 800-page report released by Governor Nathan Deals's office alleging that nearly 200 teachers and principals from 44 of the district's schools cheated on required standardized tests. Eighty-two of the teachers confessed to having done so. As an Associated Press story by Bob Andres, printed by *USA Today* (July 6, 2011) put it, the report showed that Atlanta emphasized test results "to the exclusion of integrity and ethics." The story went on to say that the pressure put on teachers was such that some were frightened, with one third grade teacher telling investigators that "there are ways that APS (Atlanta Public Schools) can get back at you" if you do not go along with the cheating.

The Atlanta scandal took a toll on the career of the superintendent, Dr. Beverly Hall. A highly successful superintendent of large urban districts over the years, and superintendent of the Atlanta system from 1999 until June of 2011, Dr. Hall observed in an interview published on September 2, 2011 in the *New York Times* that "I feel badly for myself, but I feel just as badly for all the people in this district who are working hard. Now everything they read and hear is negative. That is taking a tremendous toll on me." While she was not tied directly to the scandal by the Governor's report, the report stated that she had to have known about it or should have. The question that arose in her case was whether or not, by her leadership style and direction, she created a culture that inspired the cheating to meet what otherwise were significant and admirable goals—increasing the performance of the Atlanta students, especially those from challenged backgrounds.

And a scandal raising similar ethical issues surfaced in the Washington D.C. schools where the superintendent at the time, Michelle Rhee, was likewise questioned regarding whether or not she created a culture of test score competitiveness and rewards that led to cheating—discovered through a very high erasure count on student answer sheets from one school. And similar allegations plagued some schools in the Los Angeles Public Schools and the Detroit Public Schools. Principals fearing for their jobs and teachers likewise concerned, all contributed to what, at the very least, might be characterized as questionable judgment and practice and what other, harsher critics would characterize as ethical failure. Again, these incidents are not based on something clearly illegal being done, although in some cases that might have been so, but more so on a behavioral and cultural set of expectations being created that allowed for questionable behavior and judgment.

Capturing the sense of how pervasive the cheating scandals have been over the years was an article written by Lois Beckett and published by the ProPublica website on "America's Most Outrageous Teacher Cheating Scandals." Presenting a virtual hall of shame, Beckett cited eight noteworthy incidents where, even if legal implications remained in doubt, the probability of there being ethical lapses was not. The incidents started with the Lake Woebegone effect, based on Garrison Keillor's legendary town where "every child is above average," coming alive in West Virginia from 1987–89 where the state, with a very high percentage of illiteracy and poverty, was performing "above the national average" on standardized test as were students in 48 other states. This was due to them all using out of date data comparisons. Following this inauspicious beginning, in 2000, after being lauded by President for Clinton for large test score gains, a Columbus, Ohio school was alleged to have had teachers engage in cheating by giving students assistance while taking the tests. Following that was a 1999–2001 report of widespread test cheating in New York City public schools. While the report did not hold up to scrutiny, nonetheless, it cost a number of teachers and administrators their reputations. A study of cheating in Chicago's public school in the 1990s was statistically confirmed in 2002 and observed that cheating on standardized tests occurred in at least 4–5 percent of the city's schools every year. Similar kinds of scandals followed in Birmingham, Alabama in 2004, where more than 500 students who were low academic performers had been asked to leave a local high school before the administration of standardized tests but after the school received special funding based on enrollment. The other members of this "hall of shame" were Texas districts that showed irregular high and low performances from 2004–2007, a charter school with six branches in Los Angeles where the director ordered principals to break the seals on the state test to facilitate test preparation using actual questions, and the highly visible controversies in the Atlanta and Washington, D.C. schools in 2011.

And, of course, ethical lapses and even scandals are not limited to test cheating and score fixing in the schools. Financial matters are often the subject of ethical failures and, in some cases, actual criminal fraud. For example, in the Seattle, Washington area in 2011, state auditors found that $163,000 had been paid to a non-profit organization by a local school district for receipt of unverified and apparently undelivered services aimed at attracting more women and minority contractors to the school district. The non-profit was founded to help homeless and battered women. The inability to provide accountability for the funds, even though the intent of the school district may very well have been good, cost the superintendent her job. In another financial scandal, it was alleged that for over ten years in Southern California, a sports apparel and equipment company gave over $700,000 in kickbacks to high school and college coaches to purchase their products. These are but typical of the kinds of ethical questions and matters that face school districts frequently.

The Pennsylvania State University scandal noted above called attention, in a most dramatic fashion, to the potential for sexual scandals in the schools. Unfortunately, it is not too uncommon to hear reports of teachers and administrators who have had sexual relations with students and then proceeded to cover it up. And this has not been limited to male teachers and administrators alone. Some of the more controversial incidents that have attracted the attention of the media are those in which female teachers have engaged in such activities with teenage boys who are their students. While it is quite apparent that such behavior is not only unethical but also illegal, it happens nonetheless. Why? Perhaps, some would say, it is a product of human nature. On the other hand, perhaps there may be a question of the ethical tone set in the schools by the school's leaders and in their expectations for ethical behavior on the part of their colleagues.

There is no easy answer to the question of why prospective school leaders should study ethics. It is not a simple matter of right and wrong or identifying good or bad people, although that may factor into our consideration of the matter. Arguably, as has been suggested above, very few people intentionally set out to act unethically or illegally, but we know that there is unethical, and in many cases, illegal activity on the part of school leaders and their followers. Understanding ethical behavior or the lack of it and appreciating why prospective school leaders act unethically is truly a complex matter.

In this text we shall approach the study of ethics from a variety of perspectives. If we accept the premise that most, if not all, school leaders do not set out intentionally to act unethically, then we must explore why they may end up doing so. Ideally, the study of ethics would be a prescriptive listing of what can and cannot be done, and there are some elements of that to be found in how we might wish to approach the subject. School leaders come from a variety of backgrounds with different sets of cultural and religious experiences, as do their students. These experiences infuse the many ethically impacted decisions they, as school leaders, must make, and these experiences need to be taken into account.

While almost all aspiring school leaders complete course work in school law and are assumed to be knowledgeable regarding the relevant laws of their states, often with a solid background in case law, including cases from the United States Supreme Court, they have not had an opportunity to reflect on the more nuanced implications of ethical decision making. And it is that opportunity that this text hopes to provide. Consequently, keeping in mind the complexity of studying ethics and the many different experiences school leaders bring to their positions, we start with a consideration of the philosophical foundations of ethics. It is not possible or even desirable to cover every ethical philosophy that has ever been presented, but we shall consider an overview of the topic and reflect on how having a knowledge of what some of the more influential ethical philosophers throughout history have said could have relevance today. The object of such a consideration is not to have familiarity with different philosophical approaches to ethics for their own sakes, but for the purpose of helping us set our own personal ethical compass and to understand why we believe what we do, all the while displaying care and sensitivity in respecting the beliefs of those who differ from our ethical beliefs and who, as a result, might reach different ethical conclusions. Also, we need to consider our own religious and cultural values alongside the values of others who might see the world differently. It is important for us to have a frame of reference so that we can respectfully reconcile competing religious and cultural differences into our ethical decision making in the schools.

For a number of years professional and state agencies have strongly recommended, and in some cases, required that all aspiring school leaders have a working knowledge of ethical decision making and have a background that assures that they are, indeed, ethical leaders. It is important to know what these requirements are and to study the standards of the profession, from the national to the local level. Standards are not, by their definition, ethical imperatives nor are they laws, but they inform how we as school leaders should act. Failure to have an understanding of the standards of practice for the profession can be risky and can lead to poor decisions with harmful consequence for students and teachers and possible professional ruin for the leader. It is our goal to be sure that does not happen and that is why in this text we shall devote some of our consideration to the standards movement in education, with an emphasis on the ethical dimensions of those standards.

Of equal significance is the whole question of diversity in the schools and the implications this has in forming a basis for ethical decision making. There are those, no doubt, who might argue that diversity should not be a concern since ethics are the same for everyone in all circumstances. That might be the case in many circumstances but not necessarily in all. It is diversity that gives a certain life to the culture of a school and that diversity must be taken into account as the school leader assesses his or her own ethical background and expectations. This is not easy and we may leave the topic with more questions than answers, but it is a dimension of ethics that we shall want to consider carefully. Also, related to that topic is the question, "Do women school leaders see ethical decision making in a different light than male school leaders do?" There is a body of emerging research that suggests that this might be the case and it is important that we include this in our study of ethics.

In the end, however, what is most important is how we actually engage in ethical decision making and how we respond to real, school-based situations. That is why we shall devote a great deal of our reading and reflection to examining some of the more significant areas of ethical challenges in the schools as we deal with real-life case scenarios. We shall consider the kinds of problems and dilemmas we find when dealing with school finance, the possible conflict between legal requirements and ethical action, curriculum pressures, proper communication with parents and outside constituencies, personnel actions, athletics, and what we believe to be the more direct and human matters of sex, politics, and religion.

Will we answer or even address every ethical question that a school leader could face? Definitely not. But we can raise the questions and examine real-life cases that provide us with insight into how we might want to act, how we might assess how we acted, and how we might want to respond to challenges in the future.

Why do we study ethics? There is no easy and maybe even satisfactory answer. Even so, understanding our personal sense of ethics, knowing and respecting the diverse ethical views of others, and identifying criteria that allow us to serve as ethical role models for our students and colleagues will help us to become our very best and to engage in what is right and proper behavior. And it is right and proper behavior that characterize the good—in all the senses of that term—school leader.

Each chapter in this text will conclude with a series of questions entitled "Some Things to Think About." Let's get started.

Some Things to Think About

~ What do you, as an aspiring school leader, think about the need to study ethics?

~ Do you think that supposed ethical lapses by school leaders are greatly exaggerated by the media or may they actually be underreported?

~ Is there a distinction between what ethical behavior is and what legal behavior is? If so, what is that distinction and why do you think that is the case?

~ As you think about the schools with which you are most familiar, what do you see as the major ethical challenges that should be considered?

~ Do you see possible conflicts between your own sense of what ethical behavior is and what is generally believed to be accepted standards of ethical behavior in your school or district and/or society at large?

~ Is it possible for one to change his or her thinking about ethical behavior over time? Will you be able to do that or should you?

Please reflect on these questions and talk about them with your school colleagues and see what they think. Do you find that most are in agreement or is there a wide variety of responses? If there is a wide variety of responses, why do you think that is the case? On the other hand, if almost everyone responds in the same way, why do you think that is the case? Could it be that we find that there are significant differences in how people make judgments about ethical behavior or could it be that, in the end, there is a set of universal expectations regarding ethical behavior that all people share, regardless of time and place? These are among the questions and concerns that we shall explore as we move to the next chapter—Philosophical Foundations of Ethics.

References

Beckett, L. (2011). America's most outrageous teacher cheating scandals. ProPublica (September 19, 2011). Retrieved from www.propublica.org

Severson, K. (2011). A scandal of cheating, and a fall from grace. *The New York Times* (September 7, 2011).

SportsLetter (2011). Kickback scandal involving apparel company and high school coaches (May 6, 2011). Retrieved from www.sportsletter.org

Taylor, J. (2012). Paterno: "I didn't know exactly how to handle it." (January 14, 2012) Retrieved from collegefootballtalk .nbcsports.com

Toppo, G. (2011). Atlanta public school exams fudged. *USA Today* (July 6, 2011).

Young, B. (2011). School scandal: How did $163,000 end up at obscure non-profit? *The Seattle Times* (March 3, 2011).

Chapter 2

Philosophical Foundations of Ethics

Perhaps no topic in philosophy has undergone more thought and more controversy than that of ethics. What ethical behavior is has come to mean different things to different people and to different cultures. In some cultures, killing another human being is always unethical, no matter what the circumstances. In other cultures, the importance of human life is not as important. Killing another and protecting oneself and family from being killed is a whole different matter. The same could be said about the uses and abuses of private property. Some societies hold that there is no such thing as private property and that the community, as a whole, owns everything. Other societies, especially Western societies, put a premium on private property. In many ways, the acquisition and preservation of that property—including all of the activities associated with that and even using force to the extent of taking a human life—dominate all thinking about what is right and appropriate behavior.

These and many other kinds of differences in ethical thinking have been debated for centuries. Western culture calls upon the classical tradition of philosophy which focuses on developing and determining virtue in individuals and in seeing how that virtue influences right behavior. Eastern tradition, likewise, seeks to determine what is right behavior, but it often looks at the group and focuses less on individual virtue and more on communal behavior and expectations—on rules and patterns of correct behavior. In the end, though, there is really a convergence of thinking that suggests that it is possible to determine what right behavior is and to establish a sense of ethical reasoning applicable to all human beings. This is not to say that there are not different ethical standards for different times and circumstances; rather, for most of recorded human history, there have been thinkers who express a sense of right or wrong that can be used to judge behavior and to set expectations for the society in which they live.

One way to think through these differences and often changing views of what is ethical or right behavior is to take a look at some significant thinkers on the topic. And while it is not possible and maybe not even desirable to attempt to consider every philosopher who has addressed the subject, providing a reflective overview of some of the more significant ethical philosophers is of value in providing a perspective for making practical ethical decisions in the schools today.

The Classical View

The word "ethics" comes from the Greek word "ethos." According to Wikipedia, "**Ethos** is a Greek word originally meaning 'the place of living' that can be translated into English in different ways. Some possibilities are 'starting point', 'to appear', 'disposition', and from there, 'character'. From the same Greek root originates the word *ethikos*, meaning 'theory of living', and from there, the modern English word 'ethics' is derived."

This concept of the "theory of living" has been changed over time to consider the habits or "dispositions" of character for living or acting with right behavior. What this right behavior is and whether it is something that exists as a standard or set of standards independent of human nature, or is something learned, has been at the root of philosophical inquiry since the time of the Greek philosophers.

The foremost Greek thinkers to consider "right behavior" or ethical conduct are Plato (427–347 BC) who speaks through his teacher, Socrates, in the Dialogues and his pupil, Aristotle (384–322 BC). Plato is most associated with the concept of the "ideals" or the "forms"—universal constructs which exist for all time independent of matter. Plato does not address ethics *per se*, but he does discuss ethics through his many dialogues in which Socrates, his teacher, works towards attaining truth—through determined questioning—about the very nature of virtue. In the *Gorgias*, a dialogue in which Socrates points out the weakness of rhetoric over truth, Plato discusses the nature of justice, the highest of virtues, and the nature of virtue itself. In the end, this is above all others and is an ideal that is a standard of right behavior that is independent of compromising situations and motivates human beings to act honorably and correct.

In the last section of the Gorgias, Socrates states,

> *And of all that has been said, nothing remains unshaken but the saying, that to do injustice is more to be avoided than to suffer injustice, and that the reality and not the appearance of virtue is to be followed above all things, as well in public as in private life; and that when any one has been wrong in anything, he is to be chastised, and that the next best thing to a man being just is that he should become just, and be chastised and punished; also that he should avoid all flattery of himself as well as of others, of the few or of the many: and rhetoric and any other art should be used by him, and all his actions should be done always, with a view to justice.*

Justice, for Socrates and thus to Plato, his student, is the highest good.

In the *Republic* (360 BC), Plato begins this longest of his *Dialogues* with a spirited discussion with Thrasymachus on the nature of justice. Thrasymachus argues that the proper understanding of justice is that "might makes right," an argument which Socrates defeats by pointing to the concept of ideal justice that transcends "might" and is a construct that is absolute. In the *Republic*, Plato, through the voice of Socrates, gives us his famous metaphor of the cave. The truth of this metaphor, as Socrates enlightens us, is that what we see is not what is, but only a shadow of reality which exists independent of the physical world. There are ideal "forms" of all of the physical reality that gives definition to what is. Even the practice of virtue, as we see it, is but a reflection of pure virtue. Thus justice, as is the case for all of the virtues, is an ideal that only philosophy, the life of the mind, and devotion to the truth can begin to perceive. Ultimately, all thinking and behavior should strive for the contemplation of the "good," which is the source of all reality. Such a view, then, sees virtue as a set of ideal behaviors which human beings can strive to approach, but rarely get there on their own. That is why, as Plato outlines in the *Republic*, we must design a society that allows for us to more clearly see "real" truth as opposed to shadows of truth, a society led by the "philosopher kings. This metaphor is best understood by actually reading it. It can be found in Book VII of the Republic, with a major section translated by Benjamin Jowett as follows. In the dialogue, Socrates engages Glaucon in this exchange.

> **Socrates:** And now, I said, let me show in a figure how far our nature is enlightened or unenlightened: –Behold! human beings living in a underground den, which has a mouth open towards the light and reaching all along the den; here they have been from their childhood, and have their legs and necks chained so that they cannot move, and can only see before them, being prevented by the chains from turning round their heads. Above and behind them a fire is blazing at a distance, and between the fire and the prisoners there is a raised way; and you will see, if you look, a low wall built along the way, like the screen which marionette players have in front of them, over which they show the puppets.

Glaucon: I see.

Socrates: And do you see, I said, men passing along the wall carrying all sorts of vessels, and statues and figures of animals made of wood and stone and various materials, which appear over the wall? Some of them are talking, others silent.

Glaucon: You have shown me a strange image, and they are strange prisoners.

Socrates: Like ourselves, I replied; and they see only their own shadows, or the shadows of one another, which the fire throws on the opposite wall of the cave?

Glaucon: True, he said; how could they see anything but the shadows if they were never allowed to move their heads?

Socrates: And of the objects which are being carried in like manner they would only see the shadows?

Glaucon: Yes, he said.

Socrates: And if they were able to converse with one another, would they not suppose that they were naming what was actually before them?

Glaucon: Very true.

Socrates: And suppose further that the prison had an echo which came from the other side, would they not be sure to fancy when one of the passers-by spoke that the voice which they heard came from the passing shadow?

Glaucon: No question, he replied.

Socrates: To them, I said, the truth would be literally nothing but the shadows of the images.

Glaucon: That is certain.

Socrates: And now look again, and see what will naturally follow it' the prisoners are released and disabused of their error. At first, when any of them is liberated and compelled suddenly to stand up and turn his neck round and walk and look towards the light, he will suffer sharp pains; the glare will distress him, and he will be unable to see the realities of which in his former state he had seen the shadows; and then conceive some one saying to him, that what he saw before was an illusion, but that now, when he is approaching nearer to being and his eye is turned towards more real existence, he has a clearer vision, -what will be his reply? And you may further imagine that his instructor is pointing to the objects as they pass and requiring him to name them, -will he not be perplexed? Will he not fancy that the shadows which he formerly saw are truer than the objects which are now shown to him?

Glaucon: Far truer.

Socrates: And if he is compelled to look straight at the light, will he not have a pain in his eyes which will make him turn away to take and take in the objects of vision which he can see, and which he will conceive to be in reality clearer than the things which are now being shown to him?

Glaucon: True, he said.

Socrates: And suppose once more, that he is reluctantly dragged up a steep and rugged ascent, and held fast until he's forced into the presence of the sun himself, is he not likely to be pained and irritated? When he approaches the light his eyes will be dazzled, and he will not be able to see anything at all of what are now called realities.

Glaucon: Not all in a moment, he said.

Socrates: He will require to grow accustomed to the sight of the upper world. And first he will see the shadows best, next the reflections of men and other objects in the water, and then the objects themselves; then he will gaze upon the light of the moon and the stars and the spangled heaven; and he will see the sky and the stars by night better than the sun or the light of the sun by day?

Glaucon: Certainly.

Socrates: Last of he will be able to see the sun, and not mere reflections of him in the water, but he will see him in his own proper place, and not in another; and he will contemplate him as he is.

Glaucon: Certainly.

Socrates: He will then proceed to argue that this is he who gives the season and the years, and is the guardian of all that is in the visible world, and in a certain way the cause of all things which he and his fellows have been accustomed to behold?

Glaucon: Clearly, he said, he would first see the sun and then reason about him.

Socrates: And when he remembered his old habitation, and the wisdom of the den and his fellow-prisoners, do you not suppose that he would felicitate himself on the change, and pity them?

Glaucon: Certainly, he would.

Socrates: And if they were in the habit of conferring honours among themselves on those who were quickest to observe the passing shadows and to remark which of them went before, and which followed after, and which were together; and who were therefore best able to draw conclusions as to the future, do you think that he would care for such honours and glories, or envy the possessors of them? Would he not say with Homer, Better to be the poor servant of a poor master, and to endure anything, rather than think as they do and live after their manner?

Glaucon: Yes, he said, I think that he would rather suffer anything than entertain these false notions and live in this miserable manner.

Socrates: Imagine once more, I said, such as one coming suddenly out of the sun to be replaced in his old situation; would he not be certain to have his eyes full of darkness?

Glaucon: To be sure, he said.

Socrates: And if there were a contest, and he had to compete in measuring the shadows with the prisoners who had never moved out of the den, while his sight was still weak, and before his eyes had become steady (and the time which would be needed to acquire this new habit of sight might be very considerable) would he not be ridiculous? Men would say of him that up he went and down he came without his eyes; and that it was better not even to think of ascending; and if any one tried to loose another and lead him up to the light, let them only catch the offender, and they would put him to death.

Glaucon: No question, he said.

Socrates: This entire allegory, I said, you may now append, dear Glaucon, to the previous argument; the prison-house is the world of sight, the light of the fire is the sun, and you will not misapprehend me if you interpret the journey upwards to be the ascent of the soul into the intellectual world according to my poor belief, which, at your desire, I have expressed whether rightly or wrongly God knows. But, whether true or false, my opinion is that in the world of knowledge the idea of good appears last of all, and is seen only with an effort; and, when seen, is also inferred to be the universal author of all things beautiful and right, parent of light and of the lord of light in this visible world, and the immediate source of reason and truth in the intellectual; and that this is the power upon which he who would act rationally, either in public or private life must have his eye fixed.

Glaucon: I agree, he said, as far as I am able to understand you.

Socrates: Moreover, I said, you must not wonder that those who attain to this beatific vision are unwilling to descend to human affairs; for their souls are ever hastening into the upper world where they desire to dwell; which desire of theirs is very natural, if our allegory may be trusted.

Glaucon: Yes, very natural.

Socrates: And is there anything surprising in one who passes from divine contemplations to the evil state of man, misbehaving himself in a ridiculous manner; if, while his eyes are blinking and before he has become accustomed to the surrounding darkness, he is compelled to fight in courts of law, or in other places, about the images or the shadows of images of justice, and is endeavouring to meet the conceptions of those who have never yet seen absolute justice?

Glaucon: Anything but surprising, he replied.

Socrates: Any one who has common sense will remember that the bewilderments of the eyes are of two kinds, and arise from two causes, either from coming out of the light or from going into the light, which is true of the mind's eye, quite as much as of the bodily eye; and he who remembers this when he sees any one whose vision is perplexed and weak, will not be too ready to laugh; he will first ask whether that soul of man has come out of the brighter light, and is unable to see because unaccustomed to the dark, or having turned from darkness to the day is dazzled by excess of light. And he will count the one happy in his condition and state of being, and he will pity the other; or, if he have a mind to laugh at the soul which comes from below into the light, there will be more reason in this than in the laugh which greets him who returns from above out of the light into the den.

Glaucon: That, he said, is a very just distinction.

Socrates: But then, if I am right, certain professors of education must be wrong when they say that they can put a knowledge into the soul which was not there before, like sight into blind eyes.

Glaucon: They undoubtedly say this, he replied.

Socrates: Whereas, our argument shows that the power and capacity of learning exists in the soul already; and that just as the eye was unable to turn from darkness to light without the whole body, so too the instrument of knowledge can only by the movement of the whole soul be turned from the world of becoming into that of being, and learn by degrees to endure the sight of being, and of the brightest and best of being, or in other words, of the good.

Glaucon: Very true.

Socrates: And must there not be some art which will effect conversion in the easiest and quickest manner; not implanting the faculty of sight, for that exists already, but has been turned in the wrong direction, and is looking away from the truth?

Glaucon: Yes, he said, such an art may be presumed.

Socrates: And whereas the other so-called virtues of the soul seem to be akin to bodily qualities, for even when they are not originally innate they can be implanted later by habit and exercise, the [*sic*] of wisdom more than anything else contains a divine element which always remains, and by this conversion is rendered useful and profitable; or, on the other hand, hurtful and useless. Did you never observe the narrow intelligence flashing from the keen eye of a clever rogue—how eager he is, how clearly his paltry soul sees the way to his end; he is the reverse of blind, but his keen eyesight is forced into the service of evil, and he is mischievous in proportion to his cleverness.

Glaucon: Very true, he said.

Socrates: But what if there had been a circumcision of such natures in the days of their youth; and they had been severed from those sensual pleasures, such as eating and drinking, which, like leaden weights, were attached to them at their birth, and which drag them down and turn the vision of their souls upon the things that are below—if, I say, they had been released from these impediments and turned in the opposite direction, the very same faculty in them would have seen the truth as keenly as they see what their eyes are turned to now.

Glaucon: Very likely.

Socrates: Yes, I said; and there is another thing which is likely. or rather a necessary inference from what has preceded, that neither the uneducated and uninformed of the truth, nor yet those who never make an end of their education, will be able ministers of State; not the former, because they have no single aim of duty which is the rule of all their actions, private as well as public; nor the latter, because they will not act at all except upon compulsion, fancying that they are already dwelling apart in the islands of the blest.

Glaucon: Very true, he replied.

Socrates: Then, I said, the business of us who are the founders of the State will be to compel the best minds to attain that knowledge which we have already shown to be the greatest of all—they must continue to ascend until they arrive at the good; but when they have ascended and seen enough we must not allow them to do as they do now.

Glaucon: What do you mean?

Socrates: I mean that they remain in the upper world: but this must not be allowed; they must be made to descend again among the prisoners in the den, and partake of their labours and honours, whether they are worth having or not.

Glaucon: But is not this unjust? he said; ought we to give them a worse life, when they might have a better?

Socrates: You have again forgotten, my friend, I said, the intention of the legislator, who did not aim at making any one class in the State happy above the rest; the happiness was to be in the whole State, and he held the citizens together by persuasion and necessity, making them benefactors of the State, and therefore benefactors of one another; to this end he created them, not to please themselves, but to be his instruments in binding up the State.

Glaucon: True, he said, I had forgotten.

Socrates: Observe, Glaucon, that there will be no injustice in compelling our philosophers to have a care and providence of others; we shall explain to them that in other States, men of their class are not obliged to share in the toils of politics: and this is reasonable, for they grow up at their own sweet will, and the government would rather not have them. Being self-taught, they cannot be expected to show any gratitude for a culture which they have never received. But we have brought you into the world to be rulers of the hive, kings of yourselves and of the other citizens, and have educated you far better and more perfectly than they have been educated, and you are better able to share in the double duty. Wherefore each of you, when his turn comes, must go down to the general underground abode, and get the habit of seeing in the dark. When you have acquired the habit, you will see ten thousand times better than the inhabitants of the den, and you will know what the several images are, and what they represent, because you have seen the beautiful and just and good in their truth. And thus our State which is also yours will be a reality, and not a dream only, and will be administered in a spirit unlike that of other States, in which men fight with one another about shadows only and are distracted in the struggle for power, which in their eyes is a great good. Whereas the truth is that the State in which the rulers are most reluctant to govern is always the best and most quietly governed, and the State in which they are most eager, the worst.

Ethics, for Plato, then would appear to be the study of the reflections of perfect virtues and the practice of perfect or ideal behavior.

Aristotle

Aristotle, on the other hand, takes a different view and approaches the subject as based in the reality we perceive. He argues that virtue is habit and that ethics is the pursuit of personal happiness—leading and attaining the good life—through the repeated exercise of right behavior. Aristotle was a pupil of Plato and lived from 384 BC to 327 BC. In addition to his work with Plato, he was the tutor to Alexander the Great. Over time, and after Plato's death, he developed his own approach to philosophy and turned away from the idea of the forms or abstract perfections and concentrated more on what he could reason to from reality. Perhaps the most cited work from classical philosophy in any discussion of ethics today is

Aristotle's *Nicomachean Ethics* and it is imperative that we read a portion of this seminal work. While his whole discourse covers ten books, the heart of his argument—including one's disposition to virtue, the need to develop a habit of virtue, and the need to recognize virtue as a mean—can be found in Book II. The excerpt that follows is the W. D. Ross translation.

> Virtue, then, being of two kinds, intellectual and moral, intellectual virtue in the main owes both its birth and its growth to teaching (for which reason it requires experience and time), while moral virtue comes about as a result of habit, whence also its name (ethike) is one that is formed by a slight variation from the word ethos (habit). From this it is also plain that none of the moral virtues arises in us by nature; for nothing that exists by nature can form a habit contrary to its nature. For instance the stone which by nature moves downwards cannot be habituated to move upwards, not even if one tries to train it by throwing it up ten thousand times; nor can fire be habituated to move downwards, nor can anything else that by nature behaves in one way be trained to behave in another. Neither by nature, then, nor contrary to nature do the virtues arise in us; rather we are adapted by nature to receive them, and are made perfect by habit.
>
> Again, of all the things that come to us by nature we first acquire the potentiality and later exhibit the activity (this is plain in the case of the senses; for it was not by often seeing or often hearing that we got these senses, but on the contrary we had them before we used them, and did not come to have them by using them); but the virtues we get by first exercising them, as also happens in the case of the arts as well. For the things we have to learn before we can do them, we learn by doing them (e.g., men become builders by building and lyre-players by playing the lyre); so too we become just by doing just acts, temperate by doing temperate acts, brave by doing brave acts.

This is confirmed by what happens in states; for legislators make the citizens good by forming habits in them, and this is the wish of every legislator, and those who do not effect it miss their mark, and it is in this that a good constitution differs from a bad one.

Again, it is from the same causes and by the same means that every virtue is both produced and destroyed, and similarly every art; for it is from playing the lyre that both good and bad lyre-players are produced. And the corresponding statement is true of builders and of all the rest; men will be good or bad builders as a result of building well or badly. For if this were not so, there would have been no need of a teacher, but all men would have been born good or bad at their craft. This, then, is the case with the virtues also; by doing the acts that we do in our transactions with other men we become just or unjust, and by doing the acts that we do in the presence of danger, and being habituated to feel fear or confidence, we become brave or cowardly. The same is true of appetites and feelings of anger; some men become temperate and good-tempered, others self-indulgent and irascible, by behaving in one way or the other in the appropriate circumstances. Thus, in one word, states of character arise out of like activities. This is why the activities we exhibit must be of a certain kind; it is because the states of character correspond to the differences between these. It makes no small difference, then, whether we form habits of one kind or of another from our very youth; it makes a very great difference, or rather all the difference.

Since, then, the present inquiry does not aim at theoretical knowledge like the others (for we are inquiring not in order to know what virtue is, but in order to become good, since otherwise our inquiry would have been of no use), we must examine the nature of actions, namely how we ought to do them; for these determine also the nature of the states of character that are produced, as we have said. Now, that we

must act according to the right rule is a common principle
and must be assumed—it will be discussed later (i.e., both
what the right rule is, and how it is related to the other
virtues). But this must be agreed upon beforehand, that the
whole account of matters of conduct must be given in
outline and not precisely, as we said at the very beginning
that the accounts we demand must be in accordance with
the subject-matter; matters concerned with conduct and
questions of what is good for us have no fixity, any more
than matters of health. The general account being of this
nature, the account of particular cases is yet more lacking
in exactness; for they do not fall under any art or precept
but the agents themselves must in each case consider what
is appropriate to the occasion, as happens also in the art of
medicine or of navigation.

But though our present account is of this nature we must
give what help we can. First, then, let us consider this, that
it is the nature of such things to be destroyed by defect and
excess, as we see in the case of strength and of health (for to
gain light on things imperceptible we must use the evidence
of sensible things); both excessive and defective exercise
destroys the strength, and similarly drink or food which is
above or below a certain amount destroys the health, while
that which is proportionate both produces and increases
and preserves it. So too is it, then, in the case of temperance
and courage and the other virtues. For the man who flies
from and fears everything and does not stand his ground
against anything becomes a coward, and the man who fears
nothing at all but goes to meet every danger becomes rash;
and similarly the man who indulges in every pleasure and
abstains from none becomes self-indulgent, while the man
who shuns every pleasure, as boors do, becomes in a way
insensible; temperance and courage, then, are destroyed by
excess and defect, and preserved by the mean.

But not only are the sources and causes of their origination
and growth the same as those of their destruction, but also
the sphere of their actualization will be the same; for this is

also true of the things which are more evident to sense, e.g., of strength; it is produced by taking much food and undergoing much exertion, and it is the strong man that will be most able to do these things. So too is it with the virtues; by abstaining from pleasures we become temperate, and it is when we have become so that we are most able to abstain from them; and similarly too in the case of courage; for by being habituated to despise things that are terrible and to stand our ground against them we become brave, and it is when we have become so that we shall be most able to stand our ground against them.

We must take as a sign of states of character the pleasure or pain that ensues on acts; for the man who abstains from bodily pleasures and delights in this very fact is temperate, while the man who is annoyed at it is self-indulgent, and he who stands his ground against things that are terrible and delights in this or at least is not pained is brave, while the man who is pained is a coward. For moral excellence is concerned with pleasures and pains; it is on account of the pleasure that we do bad things, and on account of the pain that we abstain from noble ones. Hence we ought to have been brought up in a particular way from our very youth, as Plato says, so as both to delight in and to be pained by the things that we ought; for this is the right education.

Again, if the virtues are concerned with actions and passions, and every passion and every action is accompanied by pleasure and pain, for this reason also virtue will be concerned with pleasures and pains. This is indicated also by the fact that punishment is inflicted by these means; for it is a kind of cure, and it is the nature of cures to be effected by contraries.

Again, as we said but lately, every state of soul has a nature relative to and concerned with the kind of things by which it tends to be made worse or better; but it is by reason of pleasures and pains that men become bad, by pursuing and avoiding these, either the pleasures and pains they ought not or when they ought not or as they ought not, or by going wrong in one of the other similar ways that may be distinguished. Hence men even define the virtues as certain states of impassivity and rest; not well, however, because they speak absolutely, and do not say 'as one ought' and 'as one ought not' and 'when one ought or ought not', and the other things that may be added. We assume, then, that this kind of excellence tends to do what is best with regard to pleasures and pains, and vice does the contrary.

The following facts also may show us that virtue and vice are concerned with these same things. There being three objects of choice and three of avoidance, the noble, the advantageous, the pleasant, and their contraries, the base, the injurious, the painful, about all of these the good man tends to go right and the bad man to go wrong, and especially about pleasure; for this is common to the animals, and also it accompanies all objects of choice; for even the noble and the advantageous appear pleasant.

Again, it has grown up with us all from our infancy; this is why it is difficult to rub off this passion, engrained as it is in our life. And we measure even our actions, some of us more and others less, by the rule of pleasure and pain. For this reason, then, our whole inquiry must be about these; for to feel delight and pain rightly or wrongly has no small effect on our actions.

Again, it is harder to fight with pleasure than with anger, to use Heraclitus' phrase, but both art and virtue are always concerned with what is harder; for even the good is better when it is harder. Therefore for this reason also the whole concern both of virtue and of political science is with pleasures and pains; for the man who uses these well will be good, he who uses them badly bad.

That virtue, then, is concerned with pleasures and pains, and that by the acts from which it arises it is both increased and, if they are done differently, destroyed, and that the acts

from which it arose are those in which it actualizes itself—
let this be taken as said.

The question might be asked; what we mean by saying that
we must become just by doing just acts, and temperate by
doing temperate acts; for if men do just and temperate acts,
they are already just and temperate, exactly as, if they do
what is in accordance with the laws of grammar and of
music, they are grammarians and musicians.

Or is this not true even of the arts? It is possible to do
something that is in accordance with the laws of grammar,
either by chance or at the suggestion of another. A man will
be a grammarian, then, only when he has both done
something grammatical and done it grammatically; and this
means doing it in accordance with the grammatical
knowledge in himself.

Again, the case of the arts and that of the virtues are not
similar; for the products of the arts have their goodness in
themselves, so that it is enough that they should have a
certain character, but if the acts that are in accordance with
the virtues have themselves a certain character it does not
follow that they are done justly or temperately. The agent
also must be in a certain condition when he does them; in
the first place he must have knowledge, secondly he must
choose the acts, and choose them for their own sakes, and
thirdly his action must proceed from a firm and
unchangeable character. These are not reckoned in as
conditions of the possession of the arts, except the bare
knowledge; but as a condition of the possession of the
virtues knowledge has little or no weight, while the other
conditions count not for a little but for everything, i.e., the
very conditions which result from often doing just and
temperate acts.

Actions, then, are called just and temperate when they are
such as the just or the temperate man would do; but it is
not the man who does these that is just and temperate, but

the man who also does them as just and temperate men do them. It is well said, then, that it is by doing just acts that the just man is produced, and by doing temperate acts the temperate man; without doing these no one would have even a prospect of becoming good.

But most people do not do these, but take refuge in theory and think they are being philosophers and will become good in this way, behaving somewhat like patients who listen attentively to their doctors, but do none of the things they are ordered to do. As the latter will not be made well in body by such a course of treatment, the former will not be made well in soul by such a course of philosophy.

Next we must consider what virtue is. Since things that are found in the soul are of three kinds—passions, faculties, states of character, virtue must be one of these. By passions I mean appetite, anger, fear, confidence, envy, joy, friendly feeling, hatred, longing, emulation, pity, and in general the feelings that are accompanied by pleasure or pain; by faculties the things in virtue of which we are said to be capable of feeling these, e.g., of becoming angry or being pained or feeling pity; by states of character the things in virtue of which we stand well or badly with reference to the passions, e.g., with reference to anger we stand badly if we feel it violently or too weakly, and well if we feel it moderately; and similarly with reference to the other passions.

Now neither the virtues nor the vices are passions, because we are not called good or bad on the ground of our passions, but are so called on the ground of our virtues and our vices, and because we are neither praised nor blamed for our passions (for the man who feels fear or anger is not praised, nor is the man who simply feels anger blamed, but the man who feels it in a certain way), but for our virtues and our vices we are praised or blamed.

Again, we feel anger and fear without choice, but the virtues are modes of choice or involve choice. Further, in respect of the passions we are said to be moved, but in respect of the virtues and the vices we are said not to be moved but to be disposed in a particular way.

For these reasons also they are not faculties; for we are neither called good nor bad, nor praised nor blamed, for the simple capacity of feeling the passions; again, we have the faculties by nature, but we are not made good or bad by nature; we have spoken of this before. If, then, the virtues are neither passions nor faculties, all that remains is that they should be states of character.

Thus we have stated what virtue is in respect of its genus.

We must, however, not only describe virtue as a state of character, but also say what sort of state it is. We may remark, then, that every virtue or excellence both brings into good condition the thing of which it is the excellence and makes the work of that thing be done well; e.g., the excellence of the eye makes both the eye and its work good; for it is by the excellence of the eye that we see well. Similarly the excellence of the horse makes a horse both good in itself and good at running and at carrying its rider and at awaiting the attack of the enemy. Therefore, if this is true in every case, the virtue of man also will be the state of character which makes a man good and which makes him do his own work well.

How this is to happen we have stated already, but it will be made plain also by the following consideration of the specific nature of virtue. In everything that is continuous and divisible it is possible to take more, less, or an equal amount, and that either in terms of the thing itself or relatively to us; and the equal is an intermediate between excess and defect. By the intermediate in the object I mean that which is equidistant from each of the extremes, which is one and the same for all men; by the intermediate relatively to us that which is neither too much nor too little—and this is not one, nor the same for all. For instance, if ten is many and two is few, six is the intermediate, taken in terms of the object; for it exceeds and is exceeded by an equal amount; this is intermediate according to arithmetical proportion. But the intermediate relatively to us is not to be taken so; if ten pounds are too much for a particular person to eat and two too little, it does not follow that the trainer will order six pounds; for this also is perhaps too much for the person who is to take it, or too little—too little for Milo, too much for the beginner in athletic exercises. The same is true of running and wrestling. Thus a master of any art avoids excess and defect, but seeks the intermediate and chooses this—the intermediate not in the object but relatively to us.

If it is thus, then, that every art does its work well—by looking to the intermediate and judging its works by this standard (so that we often say of good works of art that it is not possible either to take away or to add anything, implying that excess and defect destroy the goodness of works of art, while the mean preserves it; and good artists, as we say, look to this in their work), and if, further, virtue is more exact and better than any art, as nature also is, then virtue must have the quality of aiming at the intermediate. I mean moral virtue; for it is this that is concerned with passions and actions, and in these there is excess, defect, and the intermediate. For instance, both fear and confidence and appetite and anger and pity and in general pleasure and pain may be felt both too much and too little, and in both cases not well; but to feel them at the right times, with reference to the right objects, towards the right people, with the right motive, and in the right way, is what is both intermediate and best, and this is characteristic of virtue. Similarly with regard to actions also there is excess, defect, and the intermediate. Now virtue is concerned with passions and actions, in which excess is a form of failure, and so is defect, while the intermediate is praised and is a form of success; and being praised and being successful are both characteristics of virtue. Therefore virtue is a kind of mean, since, as we have seen, it aims at what is intermediate.

Again, it is possible to fail in many ways (for evil belongs to the class of the unlimited, as the Pythagoreans conjectured, and good to that of the limited), while to succeed is possible only in one way (for which reason also one is easy and the other difficult—to miss the mark easy, to hit it difficult); for these reasons also, then, excess and defect are characteristic of vice, and the mean of virtue;

For men are good in but one way, but bad in many.

Virtue, then, is a state of character concerned with choice, lying in a mean (i.e., the mean relative to us), this being determined by a rational principle, and by that principle by which the man of practical wisdom would determine it. Now it is a mean between two vices, that which depends on excess and that which depends on defect; and again it is a mean because the vices respectively fall short of or exceed what is right in both passions and actions, while virtue both finds and chooses that which is intermediate. Hence in respect of its substance and the definition that states its essence virtue is a mean, with regard to what is best and right an extreme.

But not every action nor every passion admits of a mean; for some have names that already imply badness, e.g., spite, shamelessness, envy, and in the case of actions adultery, theft, murder; for all of these and suchlike things imply by their names that they are themselves bad, and not the excesses or deficiencies of them. It is not possible, then, ever to be right with regard to them; one must always be wrong. Nor does goodness or badness with regard to such things depend on committing adultery with the right woman, at the right time, and in the right way, but simply to do any of them is to go wrong. It would be equally absurd, then, to expect that in unjust, cowardly, and voluptuous action there should be a mean, an excess, and a deficiency; for at that rate there would be a mean of excess and of deficiency, an excess of excess, and a deficiency of deficiency. But as there is no excess and deficiency of temperance and courage because what is intermediate is in a sense an extreme, so too of the actions we have mentioned there is no mean nor any excess and deficiency, but however they are done they are wrong; for in general there is neither a mean of excess and deficiency, nor excess and deficiency of a mean.

We must, however, not only make this general statement, but also apply it to the individual facts. For among statements about conduct those which are general apply more widely, but those which are particular are more genuine, since conduct has to do with individual cases, and our statements must harmonize with the facts in these cases. We may take these cases from our table. With regard to feelings of fear and confidence courage is the mean; of the people who exceed, he who exceeds in fearlessness has no name (many of the states have no name), while the man who exceeds in confidence is rash, and he who exceeds in fear and falls short in confidence is a coward. With regard to pleasures and pains—not all of them, and not so much with regard to the pains—the mean is temperance, the excess self-indulgence. Persons deficient with regard to the pleasures are not often found; hence such persons also have received no name. But let us call them 'insensible.'

With regard to giving and taking of money the mean is liberality, the excess and the defect prodigality and meanness. In these actions people exceed and fall short in contrary ways; the prodigal exceeds in spending and falls short in taking, while the mean man exceeds in taking and falls short in spending. (At present we are giving a mere outline or summary, and are satisfied with this; later these states will be more exactly determined.) With regard to money there are also other dispositions—a mean, magnificence (for the magnificent man differs from the liberal man; the former deals with large sums, the latter with small ones), an excess, tastelessness and vulgarity, and a deficiency, niggardliness; these differ from the states opposed to liberality, and the mode of their difference will be stated later. With regard to honour and dishonour the mean is proper pride, the excess is known as a sort of 'empty vanity', and the deficiency is undue humility; and as we said liberality was related to magnificence, differing from it by dealing with small sums, so there is a state similarly related to proper pride, being concerned with small honours while that is concerned with great. For it is possible to desire honour as one ought, and more than one ought, and less, and the man who exceeds in his desires is called ambitious, the man who falls short unambitious, while the intermediate person has no name. The dispositions also are nameless, except that that of the ambitious man is called ambition. Hence the people who are at the extremes lay claim to the middle place; and we ourselves sometimes call the intermediate person ambitious and sometimes unambitious, and sometimes praise the ambitious man and sometimes the unambitious. The reason of our doing this will be stated in what follows; but now let us speak of the remaining states according to the method which has been indicated.

With regard to anger also there is an excess, a deficiency, and a mean. Although they can scarcely be said to have names, yet since we call the intermediate person good-tempered let us call the mean good temper; of the persons at the extremes let the one who exceeds be called irascible, and his vice irascibility, and the man who falls short an inirascible sort of person, and the deficiency inirascibility.

There are also three other means, which have a certain likeness to one another, but differ from one another: for they are all concerned with intercourse in words and actions, but differ in that one is concerned with truth in this sphere, the other two with pleasantness; and of this one

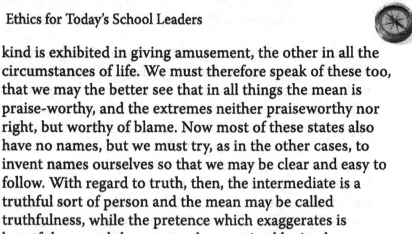

kind is exhibited in giving amusement, the other in all the
circumstances of life. We must therefore speak of these too,
that we may the better see that in all things the mean is
praise-worthy, and the extremes neither praiseworthy nor
right, but worthy of blame. Now most of these states also
have no names, but we must try, as in the other cases, to
invent names ourselves so that we may be clear and easy to
follow. With regard to truth, then, the intermediate is a
truthful sort of person and the mean may be called
truthfulness, while the pretence which exaggerates is
boastfulness and the person characterized by it a boaster,
and that which understates is mock modesty and the person
characterized by it mock-modest. With regard to
pleasantness in the giving of amusement the intermediate
person is ready-witted and the disposition ready wit, the
excess is buffoonery and the person characterized by it a
buffoon, while the man who falls short is a sort of boor and
his state is boorishness. With regard to the remaining kind
of pleasantness, that which is exhibited in life in general,
the man who is pleasant in the right way is friendly and the
mean is friendliness, while the man who exceeds is an
obsequious person if he has no end in view, a flatterer if he
is aiming at his own advantage, and the man who falls short
and is unpleasant in all circumstances is a quarrelsome and
surly sort of person.

There are also means in the passions and concerned with
the passions; since shame is not a virtue, and yet praise is
extended to the modest man. For even in these matters one
man is said to be intermediate, and another to exceed, as
for instance the bashful man who is ashamed of everything;
while he who falls short or is not ashamed of anything at all
is shameless, and the intermediate person is modest.
Righteous indignation is a mean between envy and spite,
and these states are concerned with the pain and pleasure
that are felt at the fortunes of our neighbours; the man who
is characterized by righteous indignation is pained at
undeserved good fortune, the envious man, going beyond

him, is pained at all good fortune, and the spiteful man falls so far short of being pained that he even rejoices. But these states there will be an opportunity of describing elsewhere; with regard to justice, since it has not one simple meaning, we shall, after describing the other states, distinguish its two kinds and say how each of them is a mean; and similarly we shall treat also of the rational virtues.

There are three kinds of disposition, then, two of them vices, involving excess and deficiency respectively, and one a virtue, viz. the mean, and all are in a sense opposed to all; for the extreme states are contrary both to the intermediate state and to each other, and the intermediate to the extremes; as the equal is greater relatively to the less, less relatively to the greater, so the middle states are excessive relatively to the deficiencies, deficient relatively to the excesses, both in passions and in actions. For the brave man appears rash relatively to the coward, and cowardly relatively to the rash man; and similarly the temperate man appears self-indulgent relatively to the insensible man, insensible relatively to the self-indulgent, and the liberal man prodigal relatively to the mean man, mean relatively to the prodigal. Hence also the people at the extremes push the intermediate man each over to the other, and the brave man is called rash by the coward, cowardly by the rash man, and correspondingly in the other cases.

These states being thus opposed to one another, the greatest contrariety is that of the extremes to each other, rather than to the intermediate; for these are further from each other than from the intermediate, as the great is further from the small and the small from the great than both are from the equal. Again, to the intermediate some extremes show a certain likeness, as that of rashness to courage and that of prodigality to liberality; but the extremes show the greatest unlikeness to each other; now contraries are defined as the things that are furthest from each other, so that things that are further apart are more contrary.

To the mean in some cases the deficiency, in some the excess is more opposed; for example, it is not rashness, which is an excess, but cowardice, which is a deficiency, that is more opposed to courage, and not insensibility, which is a deficiency, but self-indulgence, which is an excess, that is more opposed to temperance. This happens from two reasons, one being drawn from the thing itself; for because one extreme is nearer and more like the intermediate, we oppose not this but rather its contrary to the intermediate. For example, since rashness is thought more like and nearer to courage, and cowardice more unlike, we oppose rather the latter to courage; for things that are further from the intermediate are thought more contrary to it. This, then, is one cause, drawn from the thing itself; another is drawn from ourselves; for the things to which we ourselves more naturally tend seem more contrary to the intermediate. For instance, we ourselves tend more naturally to pleasures, and hence are more easily carried away towards self-indulgence than towards propriety. We describe as contrary to the mean, then, rather the directions in which we more often go to great lengths; and therefore self-indulgence, which is an excess, is the more contrary to temperance.

That moral virtue is a mean, then, and in what sense it is so, and that it is a mean between two vices, the one involving excess, the other deficiency, and that it is such because its character is to aim at what is intermediate in passions and in actions, has been sufficiently stated. Hence also it is no easy task to be good. For in everything it is no easy task to find the middle, e.g., to find the middle of a circle is not for every one but for him who knows; so, too, any one can get angry—that is easy—or give or spend money; but to do this to the right person, to the right extent, at the right time, with the right motive, and in the right way, that is not for every one, nor is it easy; wherefore goodness is both rare and laudable and noble.

Hence he who aims at the intermediate must first depart from what is the more contrary to it, as Calypso advises—

Hold the ship out beyond that surf and spray.

For of the extremes one is more erroneous, one less so; therefore, since to hit the mean is hard in the extreme, we must as a second best, as people say, take the least of the evils; and this will be done best in the way we describe. But we must consider the things towards which we ourselves also are easily carried away; for some of us tend to one thing, some to another; and this will be recognizable from the pleasure and the pain we feel. We must drag ourselves away to the contrary extreme; for we shall get into the intermediate state by drawing well away from error, as people do in straightening sticks that are bent.

Now in everything the pleasant or pleasure is most to be guarded against; for we do not judge it impartially. We ought, then, to feel towards pleasure as the elders of the people felt towards Helen, and in all circumstances repeat their saying; for if we dismiss pleasure thus we are less likely to go astray. It is by doing this, then, (to sum the matter up) that we shall best be able to hit the mean.

But this is no doubt difficult, and especially in individual cases; for or is not easy to determine both how and with whom and on what provocation and how long one should be angry; for we too sometimes praise those who fall short and call them good-tempered, but sometimes we praise those who get angry and call them manly. The man, however, who deviates little from goodness is not blamed, whether he do so in the direction of the more or of the less, but only the man who deviates more widely; for he does not fail to be noticed. But up to what point and to what extent a man must deviate before he becomes blameworthy it is not easy to determine by reasoning, any more than anything else that is perceived by the senses; such things depend on particular facts, and the decision rests with perception. So much, then, is plain, that the intermediate state is in all things to be praised, but that we must incline sometimes towards the excess, sometimes towards the deficiency; for so shall we most easily hit the mean and what is right.

The Post Classical View of Ethics

There have been many philosophers who considered ethical behavior in the post classical period which runs from the rise of Christianity to the modern day. St. Augustine of Hippo (350–430 AD) revived the Platonist argument, but from a theological perspective in his famous *City of God* and in his *Confessions* while St. Thomas Aquinas (1225–1274) reconciled Aristotle with medieval and contemporary Christianity through his scholastic approach to philosophy. And, while it is tempting to attempt to describe all of the many different approaches to philosophy and ethics that have been put forward since the classical period, the following philosophers have been selected for consideration because of the different approaches they offer us as we reflect upon some basic Western ethical thinking over the years.

Niccolò Machiavelli (1469–1527)

Perhaps the most influential political philosopher in the Renaissance was Niccolò Machiavelli. Machiavelli is best known for his work, *The Prince*, in which he described the acquisition and maintenance of power by a strong leader—hence, the prince. He wrote during a chaotic political time in Italy. Machiavelli believed that attaining and keeping power was the essential task of the leader, to the point that he believed that a leader is not bound by conventional ethical norms. He believed that "the ends justify the means" in attaining and maintaining power. Nonetheless, he was careful in providing guidance to the prince, commenting on the fickleness of human nature and calling on the prince to be careful in manipulating that fickleness to assure that the leader's power remained secure. For example, he wrote that while it is a good thing for the leader to be loved, if one must make a choice, it is better to be feared than loved, as fear will keep the subjects under control. If the subjects realize that the leader is relying on love as the reason to follow him or her, they will quickly abandon the leader and do whatever they want. Machiavellianism is seen as having a significant influence in politics as well as in corporate and school administration. While the term *Machiavellian* is often less than flattering, it can describe what many leaders practice under the guise of realism.

Perhaps nothing better provides an insight into Machiavelli's thinking than the following excerpt, Chapter XVII, from *The Prince* (1513). The excerpt is from the W. K. Marriott translation.

Concerning Cruelty and Clemency, and Whether It Is Better to Be Loved Than Feared

Coming now to the other qualities mentioned above, I say that every prince ought to desire to be considered clement and not cruel. Nevertheless he ought to take care not to misuse this clemency. Cesare Borgia was considered cruel; notwithstanding, his cruelty reconciled the Romagna, unified it, and restored it to peace and loyalty. And if this be rightly considered, he will be seen to have been much more merciful than the Florentine people, who, to avoid a reputation for cruelty, permitted Pistoia to be destroyed. Therefore a prince, so long as he keeps his subjects united and loyal, ought not to mind the reproach of cruelty; because with a few examples he will be more merciful than those who, through too much mercy, allow disorders to arise, from which follow murders or robberies; for these are wont to injure the whole people, whilst those executions which originate with a prince offend the individual only.

And of all princes, it is impossible for the new prince to avoid the imputation of cruelty, owing to new states being full of dangers. Hence Virgil, through the mouth of Dido, excuses the inhumanity of her reign owing to its being new, saying:

"Res dura, et regni novitas me talia cogunt Moliri, et late fines custode tueri."

(. . . against my will, my fate A throne unsettled, and an infant state, Bid me defend my realms with all my pow'rs, And guard with these severities my shores. Translated by Christopher Pitt.)

Nevertheless, he ought to be slow to believe and to act, nor should he himself show fear, but proceed in a temperate manner with prudence and humanity, so that too much confidence may not make him incautious and too much distrust render him intolerable.

Upon this a question arises: whether it be better to be loved than feared or feared than loved? It may be answered that one should wish to be both, but, because it is difficult to unite them in one person, it is much safer to be feared than loved, when, of the two, either must be dispensed with. Because this is to be asserted in general of men, that they are ungrateful, fickle, false, cowardly, covetous, and as long as you succeed they are yours entirely; they will offer you their blood, property, life, and children, as is said above, when the need is far distant; but when it approaches they turn against you. And that prince who, relying entirely on their promises, has neglected other precautions, is ruined; because friendships that are obtained by payments, and not by greatness or nobility of mind, may indeed be earned, but they are not secured, and in time of need cannot be relied upon; and men have less scruple in offending one who is beloved than one who is feared, for love is preserved by the link of obligation which, owing to the baseness of men, is broken at every opportunity for their advantage; but fear preserves you by a dread of punishment which never fails.

Nevertheless a prince ought to inspire fear in such a way that, if he does not win love, he avoids hatred; because he can endure very well being feared whilst he is not hated, which will always be as long as he abstains from the property of his citizens and subjects and from their women. But when it is necessary for him to proceed against the life of someone, he must do it on proper justification and for manifest cause, but above all things he must keep his hands off the property of others, because men more quickly forget the death of their father than the loss of their patrimony. Besides, pretexts for taking away the property are never wanting; for he who has once begun to live by robbery will always find pretexts for seizing what belongs to others; but reasons for taking life, on the contrary, are more difficult to find and sooner lapse. But when a prince is with his army, and has under control a multitude of soldiers, then it is quite necessary for him to disregard the reputation of cruelty, for without it he would never hold his army united or disposed to its duties.

Among the wonderful deeds of Hannibal this one is enumerated: that having led an enormous army, composed of many various races of men, to fight in foreign lands, no dissensions arose either among them or against the prince, whether in his bad or in his good fortune. This arose from nothing else than his inhuman cruelty, which, with his boundless valour, made him revered and terrible in the sight of his soldiers, but without that cruelty, his other virtues were not sufficient to produce this effect. And short-sighted writers admire his deeds from one point of view and from another condemn the principal cause of them. That it is true his other virtues would not have been sufficient for him may be proved by the case of Scipio, that most excellent man, not only of his own times but within the memory of man, against whom, nevertheless, his army rebelled in Spain; this arose from nothing but his too great forbearance, which gave his soldiers more license than is consistent with military discipline. For this he was upbraided in the Senate by Fabius Maximus, and called the corrupter of the Roman soldiery. The Locrians were laid waste by a legate of Scipio, yet they were not avenged by him, nor was the insolence of the legate punished, owing entirely to his easy nature. Insomuch that someone in the Senate, wishing to excuse him, said there were many men who knew much better how not to err than to correct the errors of others. This disposition, if he had been continued in the command, would have destroyed in time the fame and glory of Scipio; but, he being under the control of the Senate, this injurious characteristic not only concealed itself, but contributed to his glory.

Returning to the question of being feared or loved, I come to the conclusion that, men loving according to their own will and fearing according to that of the prince, a wise prince should establish himself on that which is in his own control and not in that of others; he must endeavour only to avoid hatred, as is noted.

Thomas Hobbes (1588–1679)

Thomas Hobbes—an English philosopher writing in the mid-seventeenth century—believed in relative, not absolute, good and evil. Wrong or evil acts are a result of man's judging before there is enough understanding or evidence for proper action. Further, in the totally mechanistic (cause-and-effect) universe of Hobbes, man cannot have true free will to act. Importantly, however, he may or may not choose to act on what his mind has "willed."

Hobbes is also the father of the belief in the "divine right of kings" or sovereign power which is necessary to preserve the state—the "Leviathan"—from the basic evil and undisciplined nature which he believes characterizes mankind. Thus, man is at his best while serving the state which in turn serves mankind with order, meaning, and preservation of both the individual and the species. In the *Leviathan* (1651), Chapter XIII, Hobbes writes,

Of the Natural Condition of Mankind as Concerning Their Felicity and Misery

NATURE hath made men so equal in the faculties of body and mind as that, though there be found one man sometimes manifestly stronger in body or of quicker mind than another, yet when all is reckoned together the difference between man and man is not so considerable as that one man can thereupon claim to himself any benefit to which another may not pretend as well as he. For as to the strength of body, the weakest has strength enough to kill the strongest, either by secret machination or by confederacy with others that are in the same danger with himself.

And as to the faculties of the mind, setting aside the arts grounded upon words, and especially that skill of proceeding upon general and infallible rules, called science, which very few have and but in few things, as being not a native faculty born with us, nor attained, as prudence, while we look after somewhat else, I find yet a greater equality amongst men than that of strength. For prudence is but experience, which equal time equally bestows on all men in those things they equally apply themselves unto. That which may perhaps make such equality incredible is but a vain conceit of one's own wisdom, which almost all men think they have in a greater degree than the vulgar; that is, than all men but themselves, and a few others, whom by fame, or for concurring with themselves, they approve. For such is the nature of men that howsoever they may acknowledge many others to be more witty, or more eloquent or more learned, yet they will hardly believe there be many so wise as themselves; for they see their own wit at hand, and other men's at a distance. But this proveth rather that men are in that point equal, than unequal. For there is not ordinarily a greater sign of the equal distribution of anything than that every man is contented with his share.

From this equality of ability ariseth equality of hope in the attaining of our ends. And therefore if any two men desire the same thing, which nevertheless they cannot both enjoy, they become enemies; and in the way to their end (which is principally their own conservation, and sometimes their delectation only) endeavour to destroy or subdue one another. And from hence it comes to pass that where an invader hath no more to fear than another man's single power, if one plant, sow, build, or possess a convenient seat, others may probably be expected to come prepared with forces united to dispossess and deprive him, not only of the fruit of his labour, but also of his life or liberty. And the invader again is in the like danger of another.

And from this diffidence of one another, there is no way for any man to secure himself so reasonable as anticipation; that is, by force, or wiles, to master the persons of all men he can so long till he see no other power great enough to endanger him: and this is no more than his own conservation requireth, and is generally allowed. Also, because there be some that, taking pleasure in contemplating their own power in the acts of conquest, which they pursue farther than their security requires, if others, that otherwise would be glad to be at ease within modest bounds, should not by invasion increase their power, they would not be able, long time, by standing only on their defence, to subsist. And by consequence, such augmentation of dominion over men being necessary to a man's conservation; it ought to be allowed him.

Again, men have no pleasure (but on the contrary a great deal of grief) in keeping company where there is no power able to overawe them all. For every man looketh that his companion should value him at the same rate he sets upon himself, and upon all signs of contempt or undervaluing naturally endeavours, as far as he dares (which amongst them that have no common power to keep them in quiet is far enough to make them destroy each other), to extort a greater value from his contemners, by damage; and from others, by the example.

So that in the nature of man, we find three principal causes of quarrel. First, competition; secondly, diffidence; thirdly, glory.

The first maketh men invade for gain; the second, for safety; and the third, for reputation. The first use violence, to make themselves masters of other men's persons, wives, children, and cattle; the second, to defend them; the third, for trifles, as a word, a smile, a different opinion, and any other sign of undervalue, either direct in their persons or by reflection in their kindred, their friends, their nation, their profession, or their name.

Hereby it is manifest that during the time men live without a common power to keep them all in awe, they are in that condition which is called war; and such a war as is of every man against every man. For war consisteth not in battle only, or the act of fighting, but in a tract of time, wherein the will to contend by battle is sufficiently known: and therefore the notion of time is to be considered in the nature of war, as it is in the nature of weather. For as the nature of foul weather lieth not in a shower or two of rain, but in an inclination thereto of many days together: so the nature of war consisteth not in actual fighting, but in the known disposition thereto during all the time there is no assurance to the contrary. All other time is peace.

Whatsoever therefore is consequent to a time of war, where every man is enemy to every man, the same consequent to the time wherein men live without other security than what their own strength and their own invention shall furnish them withal. In such condition there is no place for industry, because the fruit thereof is uncertain: and consequently no culture of the earth; no navigation, nor use of the commodities that may be imported by sea; no commodious building; no instruments of moving and removing such things as require much force; no knowledge of the face of the earth; no account of time; no arts; no letters; no society; and which is worst of all, continual fear, and danger of violent death; and the life of man, solitary, poor, nasty, brutish, and short.

It may seem strange to some man that has not well weighed these things that Nature should thus dissociate and render men apt to invade and destroy one another: and he may therefore, not trusting to this inference, made from the passions, desire perhaps to have the same confirmed by experience. Let him therefore consider with himself: when taking a journey, he arms himself and seeks to go well accompanied; when going to sleep, he locks his doors; when even in his house he locks his chests; and this when he knows there be laws and public officers, armed, to revenge all injuries shall be done him; what opinion he has of his fellow subjects, when he rides armed; of his fellow citizens, when he locks his doors; and of his children, and servants, when he locks his chests. Does he not there as much accuse mankind by his actions as I do by my words? But neither of us accuses man's nature in it. The desires, and other passions of man, are in themselves no sin. No more are the actions that proceed from those passions till they know a law that forbids them; which till laws be made they cannot know, nor can any law be made till they have agreed upon the person that shall make it.

It may peradventure be thought there was never such a time nor condition of war as this; and I believe it was never generally so, over all the world: but there are many places where they live so now. For the savage people in many places of America, except the government of small families, the concord whereof dependeth on natural lust, have no government at all, and live at this day in that brutish manner, as I said before. Howsoever, it may be perceived what manner of life there would be, where there were no

common power to fear, by the manner of life which men
that have formerly lived under a peaceful government use
to degenerate into a civil war.

But though there had never been any time wherein
particular men were in a condition of war one against
another, yet in all times kings and persons of sovereign
authority, because of their independency, are in continual
jealousies, and in the state and posture of gladiators, having
their weapons pointing, and their eyes fixed on one
another; that is, their forts, garrisons, and guns upon the
frontiers of their kingdoms, and continual spies upon their
neighbours, which is a posture of war. But because they
uphold thereby the industry of their subjects, there does
not follow from it that misery which accompanies the
liberty of particular men.

To this war of every man against every man, this also is
consequent; that nothing can be unjust. The notions of
right and wrong, justice and injustice, have there no place.
Where there is no common power, there is no law; where
no law, no injustice. Force and fraud are in war the two
cardinal virtues. Justice and injustice are none of the
faculties neither of the body nor mind. If they were, they
might be in a man that were alone in the world, as well as
his senses and passions. They are qualities that relate to
men in society, not in solitude. It is consequent also to the
same condition that there be no propriety, no dominion, no
mine and thine distinct; but only that to be every man's that
he can get, and for so long as he can keep it. And thus much
for the ill condition which man by mere nature is actually
placed in; though with a possibility to come out of it,
consisting partly in the passions, partly in his reason.

The passions that incline men to peace are: fear of death;
desire of such things as are necessary to commodious
living; and a hope by their industry to obtain them. And
reason suggesteth convenient articles of peace upon which
men may be drawn to agreement. These articles are they

which otherwise are called the laws of nature, whereof I shall speak more particularly in the two following chapters.

As we see, Hobbes, not unlike Machiavelli, has a rather pessimistic view of human nature. He sees humans living in a state of uncivilized nature in a state of war, and thus living a life which is short, nasty, and brutish. It is only by force of civilization which Hobbes saw as being present in Europe and in the English monarchy to which he submitted; that this nasty state of nature can be tamed. In fact, Hobbes has been severely criticized by later writers for suggesting that, while a war-filled chaotic state of nature did not exist in most places in his time, it did, he thought, exist among the indigenous peoples in the New World. Hobbes believed that there was a need for a monarch who imposed and enforced order upon the people who, essentially, forfeited their rights to live in a community not constantly at war. Of course, we know that did not always work out well, especially as monarchs engaged in wars against rebellions within their kingdoms and against other monarchs, something Hobbes did acknowledge in this chapter. The Hobbesian view of the world, it can be argued, can lead us to an ethical point of view that relies on strong, maybe even repressive leadership, to prevent the chaos of the state of war that one might find without strong rules and regulations and harsh punishments.

What does this have to do with school leadership? In some ways it is an ethical theory that suggests that what is needed, especially in a troubled school, is an authoritarian school leader with zero tolerance for any possible threat to the running of an orderly school. There may, in fact, be school leaders today who use this approach, albeit in a more diplomatic way, and run what is known as a "tight ship."

Immanuel Kant (1724–1804)
The great German thinker of the late 18th century, Kant, formulated the philosophy that man can only know for certain what

he experiences via sensory channels. Through *Reason*, however, we can form an *Idea* of the world we inhabit by observing laws of nature and consequently construct the existence of things we cannot directly see. Kant therefore reasoned to the existence of God and all that is good, giving us an "imperative"—a "categorical imperative"—that man must act on in the belief that the "Idea" does exist. In fact, Kant's "categorical imperative" can be stated, "Always act so that you can will the maximum or determining principle of your action to become universal law; act so that you can will that everybody shall follow the principle of your action."

The "categorical imperative" allows humankind to know that slavery is wrong or that an atrocity like the Holocaust is immoral and that it would be so for all people at all times, and that these actions, in the end, are prohibited by universal law. What is not accounted for, though, is the fact that horrible things do happen in spite of what an enlightened ethicist knows is universal law.

Kant's theory of the categorical imperative is complex. It is primarily defined in Kant's *Fundamental Principles of the Meta Physics of Morals*. An especially relevant section from the beginning of this treatise follows.

We shall therefore have to investigate a priori the possibility of a categorical imperative, as we have not in this case the advantage of its reality being given in experience, so that [the elucidation of] its possibility should be requisite only for its explanation, not for its establishment. In the meantime it may be discerned beforehand that the categorical imperative alone has the purport of a practical law; all the rest may indeed be called principles of the will but not laws, since whatever is only necessary for the attainment of some arbitrary purpose may be considered as in itself contingent, and we can at any time be free from the precept if we give up the purpose; on the contrary, the unconditional command leaves the will no liberty to choose the opposite; consequently it alone carries with it that necessity which we require in a law.

Secondly, in the case of this categorical imperative or law of morality, the difficulty (of discerning its possibility) is a very profound one. It is an a priori synthetical practical proposition;* and as there is so much difficulty in discerning the possibility of speculative propositions of this kind, it may readily be supposed that the difficulty will be no less with the practical.

*I connect the act with the will without presupposing any condition resulting from any inclination, but a priori, and therefore necessarily (though only objectively, i.e., assuming the idea of a reason possessing full power over all subjective motives). This is accordingly a practical proposition which does not deduce the willing of an action by mere analysis from another already presupposed (for we have not such a perfect will), but connects it immediately with the conception of the will of a rational being, as something not contained in it.

In this problem we will first inquire whether the mere conception of a categorical imperative may not perhaps supply us also with the formula of it, containing the proposition which alone can be a categorical imperative; for even if we know the tenor of such an absolute command, yet how it is possible will require further special and laborious study, which we postpone to the last section.

When I conceive a hypothetical imperative, in general I do not know beforehand what it will contain until I am given the condition. But when I conceive a categorical imperative, I know at once what it contains. For as the imperative contains besides the law only the necessity that the maxims* shall conform to this law, while the law contains no conditions restricting it, there remains nothing but the general statement that the maxim of the action should conform to a universal law, and it is this conformity alone that the imperative properly represents as necessary.

*A maxim is a subjective principle of action, and must be distinguished from the objective principle, namely, practical law. The former contains the practical rule set by reason according to the conditions of the subject (often its ignorance or its inclinations), so that it is the principle on which the subject acts; but the law is the objective principle valid for every rational being, and is the principle on which it ought to act that is an imperative.

There is therefore but one categorical imperative, namely, this: Act only on that maxim whereby thou canst at the same time will that it should become a universal law.

Now if all imperatives of duty can be deduced from this one imperative as from their principle, then, although it should remain undecided what is called duty is not merely a vain notion, yet at least we shall be able to show what we understand by it and what this notion means.

Since the universality of the law according to which effects are produced constitutes what is properly called nature in the most general sense (as to form), that is the existence of things so far as it is determined by general laws, the imperative of duty may be expressed thus: Act as if the maxim of thy action were to become by thy will a universal law of nature.

———

For a school leader, Kant's ethical theories suggest that there are certain things that are always the right things to do. In his categorical imperative, he gives us a rational way to determine what those things are, and he moves the leader to have a firmer and more fixed set of core ethical beliefs that will guide his or her decision making process. When confronted by an ethical dilemma, the leader can reach into himself or herself to discern what is the right thing without stressing over the compromises that others might face.

John Rawls (1921–2002)

John Rawls is considered one of the most influential political and moral philosophers of the twentieth century. He is an American philosopher who has contributed greatly to considering the role of social justice in our ethical decision making. He has discussed the concepts of justice and fairness at great length, most notably in his major work, *The Theory of Justice* (1971). In this work he argues, as noted in the Cambridge Dictionary of Philosophy (1999), that "the most reasonable principles of justice are those everyone would accept and agree to from a fair position." He says that everyone should adopt what he calls the "veil of ignorance" in making decisions, asserting that no one should have an advantage, especially from his or her social or economic status, in determining what is right or proper because of that status. We need to approach judgments about social needs as though we are all equals. One can get a sense of his philosophy from the following excerpt from the Stanford Encyclopedia of Philosophy.

Two Guiding Ideas of Justice as Fairness

Social cooperation in some form is necessary for citizens to be able to lead a decent life. Yet citizens are not indifferent to how the benefits and burdens of cooperation will be divided amongst them. Rawls's principles of justice as fairness embody the central liberal ideas that cooperation should be fair to all citizens regarded as free and equal. The distinctive interpretation that Rawls gives to these concepts can be seen in broad terms as a combination of a negative and a positive thesis.

The negative thesis is that citizens do not deserve to be born into a rich or a poor family, to be born naturally more gifted than others, to be born male or female, to be born a member of a particular racial group, and so on. Since these features of persons are in this sense morally arbitrary, citizens are not at the deepest level entitled to more or less of the benefits of social cooperation because of them. For example the fact that a citizen was born rich, white, and male in itself generates no reasons for this citizen to be either favored or disfavored by social institutions.

This negative thesis does not in itself say how social goods should be distributed; it merely clears the decks. Rawls's positive distributive thesis is equality-based reciprocity. All social goods are to be distributed equally, unless an unequal distribution would be to everyone's advantage. The guiding idea is that since citizens are fundamentally equal, reasoning about justice should begin from a presumption that cooperatively-produced goods should be equally divided. Justice then requires that any inequalities must benefit all citizens, and particularly must benefit those who will have the least. Equality sets the baseline; from there any inequalities must improve everyone's situation, and especially the situation of the worst-off. These strong requirements of equality and reciprocal advantage are hallmarks of Rawls's theory of justice.

The Two Principles of Justice as Fairness

These guiding ideas of justice as fairness are expressed in its two principles of justice:

First Principle: Each person has the same indefeasible claim to a fully adequate scheme of equal basic liberties, which scheme is compatible with the same scheme of liberties for all;

Second Principle: Social and economic inequalities are to satisfy two conditions:

   a. They are to be attached to offices and positions open to all under conditions of *fair equality of opportunity*;

b. They are to be to the greatest benefit of the least-advantaged members of society (the *difference principle*). (*JF*, pp. 42–43)

The first principle of equal basic liberties is to be used for designing the political constitution, while the second principle applies primarily to social and economic institutions. Fulfillment of the first principle takes priority over fulfillment of the second principle, and within the second principle fair equality of opportunity takes priority over the difference principle.

The first principle affirms for all citizens familiar basic rights and liberties: liberty of conscience and freedom of association, freedom of speech and liberty of the person, the right to vote, to hold public office, to be treated in accordance with the rule of law, and so on. The principle ascribes these rights and liberties to all citizens equally. Unequal rights would not benefit those who would get a lesser share of rights, so justice requires equal rights for all in all normal circumstances.

Rawls's first principle accords with widespread convictions about the importance of equal basic rights and liberties. Two further features make this first principle distinctive. First, its priority: the basic rights and liberties are not to be traded off against other social goods like economic efficiency. The first principle disallows, for instance, a policy that would give draft exemptions to college students on the grounds that educated civilians will be more valuable to the economy. The draft is a drastic infringement on basic liberties, and if a draft is implemented then all who are able to serve must be equally subject to it.

The second distinctive feature of Rawls's first principle is that it requires *fair value of the political liberties*. The political liberties are a subset of the basic liberties, concerned with the right to hold public office, the right to affect the outcome of national elections, and so on. For these liberties, Rawls requires that citizens be not only formally but also substantively equal. That is, citizens similarly endowed and motivated should have the same opportunities to hold office, to influence elections, and so on regardless of their social class. This fair value proviso has major implications for how elections should be funded and run, as described below.

Rawls's second principle of justice has two parts. The first part, fair equality of opportunity, requires that citizens with the same talents and willingness to use them have the same educational and economic opportunities regardless of whether they were born rich or poor. "In all parts of society there are to be roughly the same prospects of culture and achievement for those similarly motivated and endowed." (*JF*, p. 44) So, for example, if we assume that natural endowments and willingness are evenly distributed across children born within the different social classes, then within any type of occupation (generally specified) we should find that roughly one quarter of people in that occupation were born into the top 25% of the income distribution, one quarter were born into the second-highest 25% of the income distribution, and so on. Since class of origin is a morally arbitrary fact about citizens, justice does not allow class of origin to turn into unequal real opportunities for education or meaningful work.

The second part of the second principle is the difference principle. The difference principle requires that social institutions be arranged so that inequalities of wealth and income work to the advantage of those who will be worst off. Starting from an imagined baseline of equality, a greater total product can be generated by allowing inequalities in wages and salaries: higher wages can cover the costs of training and education, for example, and can provide incentives to fill jobs that are more in demand. The difference principle requires that inequalities which increase the total product be to everyone's advantage, and specifically to the greatest advantage of those advantaged least.

Consider four hypothetical economic structures A–D, and the lifetime-average levels of income these would produce for representative members of three different groups:

Economy	Least-Advantaged Group	Middle Group	Most-Advantaged Group
A	10,000	10,000	10,000
B	12,000	15,000	20,000
C	20,000	30,000	50,000
D	17,000	50,000	100,000

Here the difference principle selects Economy C, because it contains the distribution where the least-advantaged group does best. Inequalities in C are to everyone's advantage relative to an equal division (Economy A), and a more equal division (Economy B). But the difference principle does not allow the rich to get richer at the expense of the poor (Economy D). The difference principle embodies equality-based reciprocity: from an egalitarian baseline it requires inequalities that are good for all, and particularly for the worst-off.

The difference principle gives expression to the idea that natural endowments are undeserved. A citizen does not merit more of the social product simply because she was lucky enough to be born with gifts that are in great demand. Yet this does not mean that everyone must get the same shares. The fact that citizens have different talents and abilities can be used to make everyone better off. In a society governed by the difference principle, citizens regard the distribution of natural endowments as an asset that benefits all. Those better endowed are welcome to use their gifts to make themselves better off, so long as their doing so also contributes to the

good of those less well endowed. "In justice as fairness," Rawls
says, "men agree to share one another's fate." (*TJ*, p. 102)

For the educational leader, Rawls's approach represents
some challenges regarding addressing inequality in the
schools—not only in student talent but also in terms of resources and opportunities. Arguably, society must have a
concern for the poor and the school leader might need to take
social injustice and inequity into account and, possibly, even
weigh ethical decisions in favor of those who have the most
need.

Lawrence Kohlberg

One of the foremost educational psychologists of the twentieth
century was Lawrence Kohlberg (1927–1987). Kohlberg is most
known for his theory of moral development based upon Jean
Piget's theory of cognitive development. Using research for his
doctoral dissertation, Kohlberg developed a set of stages that
children, young people, and adults go through as they develop
their moral reasoning abilities. Being aware of these stages is
important for an educational leader making ethical decisions.
Knowing where a student, parent, or community member
might be in his or her ethical/moral decision making development, as well as being aware of in what stage the leader himself
or herself might be, could have a significant influence on the
kinds of ethical decisions made by the leader or on the ethical
expectations the leader might have for the students, parents,
and community members with whom he or she comes into
contact.

Kohlberg's Stages of Moral Development follows.

Preconventional

1. Punishment—Obedience orientation; the child obeys
    because the adult or authority makes the rules and
    punishes the wrongdoer because breaking the rule is
    wrong.

2. Personal reward orientation; also seen as individualism and exchange, with a concern for meeting one's personal needs

Conventional

1. Good Boy—Nice Girl orientation; a concern for establishing relationships and being nice to preserve order, to conform to the group norms.

2. Law and Order orientation; extending relationships to a larger society and looking for keeping order based on what is fair and just.

Postconventional

1. Social contract orientation; interrelating individual and societal needs with individuals coming together to make rules for the good of all, taking into account the different cultural and moral values people have.

2. Universal ethical principal orientation; there are ethical principles that transcend societal demands and individuals engage in moral reasoning and draw upon the abstract, possibly placing them at odds with the rules and regulations of society.

～～～

Kohlberg's theory of moral development suggests that we develop morally and this development is in stages. Like Piaget's theory, we must develop a moral reasoning capacity at a lower level before we can progress to a higher level. Kohlberg's theory suggests that ethical reasoning can be taught and that one can ascend to a higher plateau of moral reasoning, such as accepting universal principles that apply to all humanity as opposed to being locked into a lower level fearing punishment or seeking being recognized as being "good' or "nice' or living at the level of law and order.

Kohlberg argues that most people get to the law and order stage and stop developing. That is the level of governments and the level of following school rules. Perhaps striving for a higher level of ethics in the schools and perhaps in government and school administration will prove to be frustrating and may not even be practical.

The Religious Perspective

Besides the classical and post-classical philosophical consideration of ethics, there is also the religious perspective. A religious sense of ethics is often at the core of people's beliefs about ethical behavior. In the United States and most western countries, with a significant number of people participating in the Judeo–Christian tradition, the Bible is used to define ethical behavior. There are different ethical perspectives in the Old and New Testaments, with the Old Testament being more legalistic in orientation and more authority driven, while the New Testament is more person and compassion oriented. And, for the most part, this tradition centers on individual responsibilities in relationship to a divine order, although there are shadings of difference regarding whether or not individual rights are more important than social responsibilities. These differences can be found among different Christian and Jewish denominations, and in the United States they spill over into divided political views of what is right and wrong.

Other religious perspectives on ethics can be found in the Quran and the sacred writings of the Eastern mystics and philosophers. Although there are many similarities in the ethical directions these religious orientations present, there are differences. With the significant diversity found in our schools, a leader must be sensitive to these different religious perspectives as well. A person from the Islamic tradition or a Hindu tradition, for example, might respond to an ethical problem in a different manner than a person whose faith is rooted in the Judeo-Christian tradition. And while it might not be possible to be completely conversant with the ethical orientations of traditions different from one's own, the educational leader must be ready to consider that his or her personal religious orientation may not be the only perspective to consider when making a decision with ethical implications.

There can be little doubt that one's religious views have profound effect on one's ethical dimensions and it would be most inappropriate to suggest that school leaders should leave their personal beliefs at the door. That being said, however, a school leader in a diverse setting will be faced with making ethical decisions that may not always follow a prescribed philosophical or religious set of principles. In the end, one should remain true to who he or she is—with a strong sense of his or her philosophical and religious beliefs—and use what might be called a personal ethical compass. That compass, discovered after thoughtful study and reflection, can give us direction and guidance grounded in our fundamental beliefs of who and what we are as ethical educational leaders.

Some Things to Think About

~ What do you think of Plato's concept of virtue—and its implications for ethical decision making—as being absolute and independent of the shadows of human experience?

~ Based on your reading of the excerpt of Aristotle's *Nichomachean Ethics*, can you describe one or more important points made by Aristotle and then discuss how these points might apply to a future school administrator's thinking about ethics today?

~ Can reaching an ultimate virtuous "end," as Machiavelli suggests, ever justify cruel or unjust "means" to attain it?

~ What implications might Hobbes's philosophy have on the running of a school or a district? What would be the pros and cons of his view? Do you know of educators who seem to be Hobbesian?

~ Can you think of an educational setting in which an individual might act on Kant's "categorical imperative"?

~ After considering Rawls's treatment of justice and fairness, can you see its relevance to the challenges an educational leader faces in addressing the issues he or she confronts in an underfunded, resource-strapped diverse school environment?

~ Do you see evidence of Kohlberg's stages of moral development in your students, colleagues, and school leaders? Could you lead a school if most people were at the universal/ethical orientation stage?

~ Now that you have read information about and/or selections from Plato, Aristotle, Machiavelli, Hobbes, Kant, Rawls, and Kohlberg, which philosophy do you see as having the most relevance in your work as a school leader? Why did you choose that philosophy and/or philosophies?

~ Is it possible that all of the philosophies make some contribution to the development of your own personal ethical compass or should some be rejected?

~ What role should a school leader's personal religious beliefs concerning ethics play in his or her educational leadership activities and decisions? Do you see any conflict between your personal religious views and your sense of how ethical decisions should be made in your school setting?

References

Aristotle (350 BC). Nicomachean ethics, Book II (translated by W. D. Ross). From Stevenson, D. Web atomics. The internet classics archives. Retrieved from Classics.mit.edu /Aristotle/nichomachean.html

Asscher, S. (e-text Editor). Plato, Gorgias, Part 4 (translated by Benjamin Jowett). Retrieved from Full Books.com

Audi, R. (Ed.) (1999). "Rawls, John." Cambridge University Press, pp. 774–775. *The Cambridge dictionary of philosophy* (2nd ed.). Cambridge, United Kingdom. Cambridge University Press, 1999.

Cherry, K. (2012). Kohlberg's theory of moral development. Stages of moral development. Retrieved from About.com .psychology

Hobbes, T. (1651). The leviathan. Retrieved from oregon state university.edu

Kant, I. (1785). "Transition from Popular Moral Philosophy to the Metaphysics of Morals." Fundamental principles of the metaphysics of morals (translated by Thomas Kingsmill Abbott). Retrieved from http://philosophye.servr.org/Kant /metaphysics

Machiavelli, N. (1513). The Prince (translated by W. K. Marriott). Fordham University. New York, NY. Internet medieval source book. Retrieved from halsall@murray .fordham.edu

Plato (380 BC). The Gorgias (translated by Benjamin Jowett, 1871). The internet classics archives. Retrieved from classics .mit.edu

Plato (360 BC). The Republic (translated by Benjamin Jowett, 1871). The internet classics archives. Retrieved from classics .mit.edu

Wenar, L. (2008). "John Rawls." The Stanford encyclopedia of philosophy (fall 2008 ed.). Zalta, E. N. (Ed.). Retrieved from URL = http://11 plato.stanford.edu/archivist fall 2008 /entries/rawls/

References

Aristotle 350 BC, Nicomachean Ethics, Book II, translated by W. D. Ross, Evans, Hugh, Stevenson, D. Watt, Stone, Thomas eds Classic Archives, Retrieved from Classicarchive.html

Berlin, I. (1998) Ethical Plato, Chapter xvii, translated by Benjamin Jowett) Retrieved from Full Books.com

Audi, R. (Ed) (1995) "The St. Louis Encyclopedia Library of Press, pp. 794–795. The Cambridge Dictionary of Philosophy (2nd ed.) Cambridge United Kingdom, Cambridge University Press, 1995.

Cherry, K. (2017) Kohlberg's Theory of moral development Stages of moral development. Retrieved from About.com Psychology.

Jones, T. (2017) The Jonathan Benn' Gutenberg state jeffers.html

Kant, I. (1785) Formerly printed Four or Metaphilosophy: the Metaphysics of Morals translated I principles of the metaphysic Edmonds translated by Thomas Kingsmill Abbott, Retrieved from Gutenberg.libraryorg.w.org/w/i metaphysics.

Machiavelli, N. (1513) The Prince (translated by W. K. Marriott) Fordham University New York NY Internet prodlaw Sourcey book Retrieved from fordham.html/pd/legislation.

Plato Text II.1 The Classics translated by Benjamin Jowett, (1871) The classical Plato archives Retrieved from classics.mit.edu.

Plato (350 BC) The Republic translated by Benjamin Jowett, (1871) The internet classical archives Retrieved from classics.mit.edu.

Weston, I. (2003) John Rawls, "The Stanford encyclopedia of philosophy (fall 2003 ed.) Zalta, E.N. (Ed.) Retrieved from URL = https://plato.stanford.edu/archive/fall 2003 entries/rawls.

Chapter 3

Codes of Ethics, Principles, and Standards for School Leaders

Distinction between Codes of Ethics, Standards, and Principles

It's important to understand and distinguish between codes of ethics, standards, and principles. Codes of ethics are defined sets of rules as to what constitutes a moral life. Ethics are defined as the well-based standards of right and wrong of an individual's core beliefs and values (Troy, 2009).

Principles are accepted or professed rules of action or conduct: a person of good moral principles (Dictionary.com). Standards are qualities of attainment, often minimum, that holds organizations, agencies, and individuals accountable for compliance of their services and products (Dictionary.com).

All professions (i.e., physicians, attorneys, accountants, and educators [teachers and administrators], etc.) have developed specific codes of ethics and standards that provide accountability for their specialties, and they have provided a measurement to hold the professionals accountable. Examples may include clean water standards imposed by a local health department, clean air standards imposed by the US Department of

Environmental Quality, American Bar Association standards that govern the practice of law for attorneys, or American Medical Association standards that govern the practice of medicine for physicians.

Although there are too many examples to cite in this chapter, one visible and notable example may apply to local city or municipality building codes imposed on a general contractor for building a home or commercial building, which ranges from structural framing requirements (foundation, framing, and roof) to plumbing and electrical requirements that promote safety comfort and reliability for the residents or tenants. To enforce these standards, cities or municipalities employ full-time building inspectors to inspect the quality of work performed by the general contractor or his sub-contractors to assure compliance with building codes.

An excellent code of principles and a statement of ethics for school administrators and supervisory and confidential personnel is one developed by the Association of California School Administrators.

Principles
Statement of Ethics

A management, supervisory, or confidential school employee's behavior must conform to an ethical code. The code must be idealistic and at the same time practical, so that it can apply reasonably to all. The professional acknowledges that the schools belong to the public they serve for the purpose of providing educational opportunities to all and providing professional leadership in the school and community. This responsibility requires standards of exemplary professional conduct. It must be recognized that the professional's actions will be viewed and appraised by the community, associates, and students. To these ends, the professional subscribes to the following statements of standards.

The management, supervisory, confidential school employee:

- Makes the well being of students the fundamental element in all decision making and actions.

- Fulfills professional responsibilities with honesty and integrity.

- Supports the principle of due process and equal treatment under the law.

- Obeys local, state, and national laws and does not knowingly join or support organizations that advocate (directly or indirectly) the overthrow of the government.

- Implements the governing board of education's policies and administrative rules and regulations.

- Pursues appropriate measures to correct those laws, policies, and regulations that are not consistent with sound educational goals.

- Avoids using positions for personal gain through political, social, religious, economic, or other influence.

- Accepts academic degrees or professional certification used in relationship with professional responsibilities only from duly accredited institutions.

- Maintains the standards and seeks to improve the effectiveness of the profession through research and continuing professional development.

- Honors all contracts until fulfillment or release.

- Seeks to involve the public and keep them honestly informed.

- Recommends the employment, development, promotion, and retention of the best possible personnel to assure a quality education program.

Bill of Rights

ACSA encourages that each member be afforded:

- The right to a written description of the professional duties and responsibilities expected to be fulfilled.

- The right to a full and impartial evaluation of professional performance, including constructive counseling on a regular and continuing basis.

- The right to participate in staff "in-service" training program(s) to improve professional performance.

- The right to be furnished the reason(s) when recommended for probation, demotion, non-renewal of contract, or termination.

- The right to due process procedures including the right to be heard by the Board of Education prior to probation, demotion, non-renewal of contract, or termination.

- The right to professional assistance from professional associations.

- The right to adequate compensation for providing important, complex, and learned professional services.

- The right to input in district policy and procedure development consistent with the individual's position on the management team and the individual's unique experience and expertise.

- The right to be accorded the respect and dignity due a member of an honorable and learned profession and an individual, sensitive, human being (ACSA.Org).

Standards and Principles

Standards and principles are rough measures or benchmarks of acceptable performance. Although they may be laws or guide-lines—as in educational legislation or judicial cases—they are more specific pronouncements within a range of acceptable practices, which are enforced by administrative or judicial sanctions. For schools, standards and principles are used to measure the performance of students, teachers, classified staff, and administrators.

Standards are also the imposition of people's values. If not achieved, the responsible stakeholders are provided incentives, sanctions to try harder, or be trained (i.e., staff development) (Maxcy, pp. 22–23).

Standards can also be expressions of hope. College football fans hold their winning football teams responsible every foot-ball season to win enough games to be bowl eligible, and pref-erably win that bowl game. If the team fails to win a substantial majority of its games for a given year or more than a year, the football coach's high paying job is on the line and the coach may be fired. If the team continues to be the league champion and win higher-level bowl championships, the coach is rewarded with a substantial salary increase and a bonus, while the athletic program is often rewarded with state of the art athletic facilities from private donations.

At first blush, there seems to be little correlation between standards, principles, and ethics. Although standards and principles assume to be value neutral, fair, impartial, reasonable, and carry mutual respect, in reality they are not. Often they originate from religious or political sources or issues, and that carries a hidden agenda engaging people into certain values judging (Fish, 1999). For example, No Child Left Behind legislation sets high standards and establishing measurable goals can improve individual outcomes in education. The Act requires states to develop assessments in basic skills. However, the hidden agenda for this legislation set up a platform for most public schools to eventually fail academically because of the impossibility to achieve increased annual yearly performance requirements.

Standards and principles are supposed to be neutral for race, gender, class, religion, ethnicity, and sexual orientation, but in reality they are not. Much of that condition is due to legislation favoring some students over others (i.e., special education, gifted, Title I, etc.). However, school leaders make local school level judgments that are favorable to some students over others for a variety of reasons (i.e., petty beliefs and emotional behavior which may compromise his/her ethics).

Purpose and Sources of Standards
The purpose of these standards is to assure the general public a sense of comfort and confidence that the various professional services that are relied upon on a daily basis are held accountable for discharging their responsibilities in a responsible, safe, and quality manner. However, there are also shortcomings for these standards being imposed. In some cases, the bar on these standards may be set too low to meet the minimal threshold for assuring the quality of products and services for minimal consumer protection and safety. From an ethical and leadership perspective, these standards may discourage high quality

leadership to promote higher expectations for products and professional services. Minimal standards, in the interest of conformity and compliance, may also discourage creativity, innovation, and risk-taking to move an organization to higher levels.

The sources of these standards are most important. Frequently, advertisements or marketing efforts by small and large businesses on television, radio, newspapers, and on the Internet are measured against an approval standard that is designed to establish the confidence of the consumer for this product and service. Is the "gold standard" named in an advertisement truly an independent agency that is credible and can hold that business or professional organization accountable for quality products or services?

According to Maxcy, high leadership standards are available in history books from historic icons such as Napoleon, Gandhi, Thoreau, etc., but seem to have eluded the standard bearers of educational administration. Standards today instead have evolved from federal and state legislated guidelines (i.e., No Child Left Behind that regulates decisions of practicing administrators along with landmark court cases). At the same time, these guidelines have imposed new standards with daunting challenges for school leaders to prepare students for high-stakes testing and accountability standards (i.e., Academic Performance Index [API] and Adequate Yearly Progress [AYP]). While these standards and guidelines may have improved the academic performance for thousands of students at hundreds of schools, these standards may also become outdated because administrators will concentrate their leadership efforts to meet average performance and qualities, as opposed for striving for greatness and innovation to educate the total child (Maxcy, p. 28).

Furthermore, the continuation of these standards to measure leadership performance may push leaders into becoming performers or actors and managing a school to compete with other schools in the name of reform and entertainment. This would be opposed to genuine face-to-face with the school community, trying new ideas and taking reasonable risks to educate the total child. Such performance demands may compromise the moral and ethical side of school leadership in favor of achieving the goals' facts (i.e., API, AYP, etc.) as a result of these performances.

This chapter will examine the various standards of accountability for school leaders, the role of applying these standards for testing and measuring student and school performances, and analyzing the attitude of these standards with the challenges of moral and ethical sensitivities.

Standards for School Leaders

There is no shortage of standards for school leaders in the United States. Several professional associations have created them to measure leadership behaviors by holding school leaders accountable to their performance standards.

The most well known of all of them is the ISLLC (Interstate School Leaders Licensure Consortium) Standards that were formulated and adopted by the Chief State School Officers (usually state superintendents or commissioners) in 1996. These standards, in turn, have served as the national foundation for standards prescribing the competencies future administrators should have in a great many states in the United States. The ISLLC Standards, for example, are the foundation for the competencies currently required of new California school administrators. The main thrust of these standards is on instructional leadership with an emphasis on assessment and accountability. This reflects a change from earlier standards that focused more on management competencies such as knowledge and application of school law and finance (National University, 2007). Below are the ISLLC Standards:

Standard 1: Setting a widely shared vision for learning

An education leader promotes the success of every student by facilitating the development, articulation, implementation, and stewardship of a vision of learning that is shared and supported by all stakeholders.

Standard 2: Developing a school culture and instructional program conducive to student learning and staff professional growth

An education leader promotes the success of every student by advocating, nurturing, and sustaining a school culture and instructional program conducive to student learning and staff professional growth.

Standard 3: Ensuring effective management of the organization, operation, and resources for a safe, efficient, and effective learning environment

An education leader promotes the success of every student by ensuring management of the organization, operation, and resources for a safe, efficient, and effective learning environment.

Standard 4: Collaborating with faculty and community members, responding to diverse community interests and needs, and mobilizing community resources

An education leader promotes the success of every student by collaborating with faculty and community members, responding to diverse community interests and needs, and mobilizing community resources.

Standard 6: Understanding, responding to, and influencing the political, social, legal, and cultural contexts

An education leader promotes the success of every student by understanding, responding to, and influencing the political, social, economic, legal, and cultural context.

In addition to promoting consistent leadership behavioral standards for school leaders, the goal of the Council of Chief State School Officers was to promote effective leadership instead of school managers. While widely accepted by educational administrator professors, these standards were widely ignored by sitting school administrators out in the field. In hopes of using these standards for the purpose of teaching school leaders leadership skills and promoting quality education, professors had them published.

It was assumed that Educational Testing Service (ETS) would use these standards as a basis of testing for licensing school administrators. However, their efforts failed and these standards are not extensively used for state administrative licensing. The ISSLC Standards emphasize three major areas for school leader accountability: knowledge, dispositions, and performances a leader would utilize in professional practice.

Out of the six straightforward ISSLC Standards, Standard 5 (the ethics standard) was composed differently. It was spelled out that a "school administrator is an educational leader who promotes the success of all students by acting with integrity, fairness, and in an ethical manner" (http://www.ccsso.org/standards.html).

Standard 5: Acting with integrity, fairness, and in an ethical manner
A school administrator is an educational leader who promotes the success of all students by acting with integrity, fairness, and in an ethical manner.

Knowledge

The administrator has knowledge and understanding of:

- the purpose of education and the role of leadership in modern society

- various ethical frameworks and perspectives on ethics

- the values of the diverse school community

- professional codes of ethics

- the philosophy and history of education

Dispositions

The administrator believes in values and is committed to:

- the ideal of the common good

- the principles in the Bill of Rights

- the right of every student to a free, quality education

- bringing ethical principles to the decision making process

- subordinating one's own interest to the good of the school community

- accepting the consequences for upholding one's principles and actions

- using the influence of one's office constructively and productively in the service of all students and their families

- development of a caring school community

Performances

The administrator facilitates processes and engages in activities ensuring that he or she:

- examines personal and professional values

- demonstrates a personal and professional code of ethics

- demonstrates values, beliefs, and attitudes that inspire others to higher levels of performance

- serves as a role model

- accepts responsibility for school operations

- considers the impact of one's administrative practices on others

- uses the influence of the office to enhance the educational program rather than for personal gain

- treats people fairly, equitably, and with dignity and respect

- protects the rights and confidentiality of students and staff

- demonstrates appreciation for and sensitivity to the diversity in the school community

- recognizes and respects the legitimate authority of others

- examines and considers the prevailing values of the diverse school community

- expects that others in the school community will demonstrate integrity and exercise ethical behavior

- opens the school to public scrutiny

- fulfills legal and contractual obligations

- applies laws and procedures (http://www.ccsso .org/standards.html)

School Leader Competencies Needed for Practicing Ethics
From Standard 5 above, there are a number of competencies needed by a school administrator in order to be a successful and ethical school leader. Knowing about ethics as related to Standard 5 means a school principal needs to know and respect the diverse values of his or her school (i.e., ethnicity, culture, and unique culture of community, etc.).

Understanding rights and common good, as stated in Standard 5, imply the impact of ethical decisions on the total school community (i.e., students, parents, staff, community stakeholders, and the impact of decision making on individual stakeholder rights). The difficult decision for the school leader is deciding the correct emphasis of his/her decision. For example:

Use ethics in decision making in Standard 5 is most important but often lacking in contemporary school administrative decision making. School leaders are often under pressure from No Child Left Behind guidelines, state and district performance guidelines, and local political pressure all or in part to make the most expedient decisions that may not include ethics as the highest priority.

Accept responsibility for decision making (also in Standard 5) eliminates the mid-level school administrators' excuse for blaming higher-level administrators or the school board as the basis for their school site decisions. School principals need to be an integral member of a district management team with all administrators accepting their share of responsibility for decision making.

Develop a caring school community in Standard 5 emphasizes a caring attitude and sensitivity of individual rights on the part of a school leader. "Our best school leaders are part of a school community: teachers, staff, administrators, board members, parents, students, and members of the public. Having an educational philosophy can help a school administrator make wise and thoughtful decisions as s/he works to make a school the best it can be."

Why is This So?

People view education through the lenses of their personal experiences. By understanding and verbalizing a philosophy, an educational leader can become better at making school a successful place for teaching and learning. Building and reinforcing integral links among school culture, productive leadership, effective teaching, assessment, school culture, and community involvement are the building blocks to school success. School leaders must help their communities become more involved in combining performance, achievement, and the teaching/learning climate, in closing the gap between potential and performance, and in helping them move toward excellence in teaching and learning—to be the best that they can be (nationaluniversity.edu).

Have a personal professional code of ethics (also in Standard 5) creates an obligation on school leaders to take pause to examine his/her own personal and professional values, as well as moral and ethical values at the school, district or workplace. However, moral and ethical values should include sensitivity of religious, ethnic, and cultural diversity that would not interfere with ethical decision making. School leader religious, cultural, or ethnic biases would be unacceptable in a public school setting.

Distinctions of Standards and Principles versus Ethics

"Standards" and "principles" can be different than ethics. Ethics provide a leader with the moral compass to make decisions. Standards set goals and competencies that must be achieved and imply negative consequences of failure if they are not attained. It may, in fact, be possible to meet standards but still not act ethically (National University, EDA 650 online course shell).

An example of a case in which standards and ethics may come into conflict is the exit examination that high school students must pass in order to graduate. Exit examinations have come into question most prominently in Florida (FCAT) and California (CAHSEE). In 2003, for example, "more than 12,500 Florida high school seniors, mostly African American and Hispanic American, were expected to leave their respective high schools without obtaining their high school diploma. The diplomas were not withheld due to deficiencies in meeting high school graduation requirements but rather because of failure to pass the FCAT" (Siegel [2004], as cited in Smith, L. and Ruhl-Smith [2006]; Examining Ethics in Educational Leadership: Some Basic Thought for Professorial Analysis; AASA Journal of Scholarship and Practice, Vol. 3, No. 2. Summer, 2006).

In the spring of 2006, the California High School Exit Examination (which students were to pass if they were to receive a diploma) was challenged in court. The first decision-ruling was that the examination violated the rights of those students who did not have equal access to the level of education required to pass—primarily students from minority, ethnic, and socioeconomic backgrounds. The decision was quickly appealed and the test standards re-instated (National University, EDA 650 online course shell).

Codes of Ethics of School Leaders

As in Standards for School Leaders, there is also a plethora of Codes of Ethics. The large education organizations such as National Education Association (NEA), National Association of Elementary School Principals Association (NAESP), American Association of School Administrators (AASA), and the California Professional Standards for Educational Leaders (CPSEL) all have excellent codes of ethics for school leaders, depending on preference. Space in this chapter precludes including all of their content, and they are easily accessible in their respective web pages. However, they are more precise and different than ethical philosophy. Below are the CPSELs:

California Professional Standards for Educational Leaders (CPSEL)

Inherent in these standards and indicators is a strong commitment to cultural diversity and the use of technology as a powerful tool. A school administrator is an educational leader who promotes the success of all students by:

Standard 1

A school administrator is an educational leader who promotes the success of all students by facilitating the development, articulation, implementation, and stewardship of a vision of learning that is shared and supported by the school community.

- Facilitate the development of a shared vision for the achievement of all students based upon data from multiple measures of student learning and relevant qualitative indicators.

- Communicate the shared vision so the entire school community understands and acts on the school's mission to become a standards-based education system.

- Use the influence of diversity to improve teaching and learning.

- Identify and address any barriers to accomplish the vision.

- Shape school programs, plans, and activities to ensure that they are integrated, articulated through the grades, and consistent with the vision.

- Leverage and marshal sufficient resources, including technology, to implement and attain the vision for all students and all subgroups of students.

Standard 2

A school administrator is an educational leader who promotes the success of all students by advocating, nurturing, and sustaining a school culture and instructional program conducive to student learning and staff professional growth.

- Shape a culture in which high expectations are the norm for each student as evident in rigorous academic work.

- Promote equity, fairness, and respect among all members of the school community.

- Facilitate the use of a variety of appropriate content-based learning materials and learning strategies that recognize students as active learners, value reflection and inquiry, emphasize the quality versus the amount of student application and performance, and utilize appropriate and effective technology.

- Guide and support the long-term professional development of all staff to be consistent with the ongoing effort to improve the learning of all students, relative to the content standards.

- Provide opportunities for all members of the school community to develop and use skills in collaboration, distributed leadership, and shared responsibility.

- Create an accountability system grounded in standards-based teaching and learning.

- Utilize multiple assessments to evaluate student learning in an ongoing process focused on improving the academic performance of each student.

Standard 3

A school administrator is an educational leader who promotes the success of all students by ensuring management of the organization, operations, and resources for a safe, efficient, and effective learning environment.

- Sustain safe, efficient, clean, well-maintained, and productive school environment that nurtures student learning and supports the professional growth of teachers and support staff.

- Utilize effective and nurturing practices in establishing student behavior management systems.

- Establish school structures and processes that support student learning.

- Utilize effective systems management, organizational development, and problem-solving and decision making techniques.

- Align fiscal, human, and material resources to support the learning of all subgroups of students.

- Monitor and evaluate the program and staff.

- Manage legal and contractual agreements and records in ways that foster a professional work environment and secure privacy and confidentiality for all students and staff.

Standard 4

A school administrator is an educational leader who promotes the success of all students by collaborating with families and community members, responding to diverse community interests and needs, and mobilizing community resources.

- Recognize and respect the goals and aspirations of diverse family and community groups.

- Treat diverse community stakeholder groups with fairness and respect.

- Incorporate information about family and community expectations into school decision making and activities.

- Strengthen the school through the establishment of community, business, institutional, and civic partnerships.

- Communicate information about the school on a regular and predictable basis through a variety of media.

- Support the equitable success of all students and all subgroups of students by mobilizing and leveraging community support services.

Standard 5

A school administrator is an educational leader who
promotes the success of all students by modeling a personal
code of ethics and developing professional leadership
capacity.

- Model personal and professional ethics, integrity,
  justice, and fairness, and expect the same
  behaviors from others.

- Protect the rights and confidentiality of students
  and staff.

- Use the influence of office to enhance the
  educational program, not personal gain.

- Make and communicate decisions based upon
  relevant data and research about effective
  teaching and learning, leadership, management
  practices, and equity.

- Demonstrate knowledge of the standards-based
  curriculum and the ability to integrate and
  articulate programs throughout the grades.

- Demonstrate skills in decision making, problem
  solving, change management, planning, conflict
  management, and evaluation.

- Reflect on personal leadership practices and
  recognize their impact and influence on the
  performance of others.

- Engage in professional and personal development.

- Encourage and inspire others to higher levels of
  performance, commitment, and motivation.

- Sustain personal motivation, commitment, energy, and health by balancing professional and personal responsibilities.

Standard 6

A school administrator is an educational leader who promotes the success of all students by understanding, responding to, and influencing the larger political, social, economic, legal, and cultural context.

- Work with the governing board and district and local leaders to influence policies that benefit students and support the improvement of teaching and learning.

- Influence and support public policies that ensure the equitable distribution of resources and support for all subgroups of students.

- Ensure that the school operates consistently within the parameters of federal, state, and local laws, policies, regulations, and statutory requirements.

- Generate support for the school by two-way communication with key decision makers in the school community.

- Collect and report accurate records of school performance.

- View oneself as a leader of a team and also as a member of a larger team.

- Open the school to the public and welcome and facilitate constructive conversations about how to improve student learning and achievement.

Limitations of Imposing Pure Standards-Based Leadership

While the ISSLC Standards, considered the "gold standard," have much to say about the importance of school leaders maintaining and improving student test scores, little or nothing is stated about making schools more democratic and equitable for staff and students. Standards do not tend to support transformational school leadership for introducing or maintaining equitable and just conditions for students.

Even though Standard 5 addresses ethics, there is no clarity on the sources of ethical values for school leaders, and no instructions as to how ethical decisions should be made. Standards-based leadership is also welcome in some states for the licensure of school administrators and promoted by Education Testing Service (ETS), but there seems to be a de-emphasis on school leaders as moral leaders (Maxcy, p. 34).

According to Marshall, there is a tendency for standards to ignore or push aside root problems in schools, leading to a naïve assumption that standards have solved all of the issues and controversies and that no new ones can arise. It appears that this phenomenon is leading to a reduced scope of school administrator decision making. School leaders should be diligent to critique and handle problems and controversies, which will improve standards via critical thinking and innovation. Without these leadership efforts, standards become obsolete and ineffective, new school and student problems and controversies remain unsolved, and the changing needs of students are not addressed.

Since the passage of No Child Left Behind legislation, there has become a national obsession with measurement and testing, in the form of standardized testing. Peter Sacks states "standardized testing has led to standardized minds." Under this assessment, students are compared with other students in a bell-shaped curve, which has led to ability groupings (Sacks, 2001). Average performances are created, spreading doubt about children who fall below that average, along with their teachers and the school principal. The result is that standardized tests have bred accountability raising questions as to why half of the student population is inadequate because their scores are below the top half of the students.

Combining Moral Character and Standards-Based Leadership Decisions

While there are strong arguments on basing decisions on standards to maintain consistency for all students and staff, school leaders should exercise their moral and ethical character, be aware of all circumstances, and should be free to choose from options including standards to make the most fair and ethical decision that is in the best interest of students. Eventually, each decision making attitude toward moral and ethical decision making establishes a school leader's character and generates their respect, integrity, and reputation among all stakeholders in the school community.

There is no question that teachers, counselors, school board members, or school leaders who lie, cheat, steal, show dishonesty, deception or theft, as well as those who show excessive cultural, ethnic, religious, or gender bias are ill-suited to be school leaders or to have any direct contact with students. These people would have been prepared for decent moral and ethical leadership if they had learned the virtues of good moral and ethical living (Maxcy, p. 36).

In earlier years, principals' leadership was considered adequate by being a school site manager (i.e., budget maintenance, scheduling, student discipline, etc.). For effective moral and ethical leadership today, principals must have a vision for the school, which determines the direction that the school should move. The vision can belong solely to the principal, but typically will have much more support if developed by a group of people.

Typically, a successful vision is the result of a strategic plan—either at the district level, site level, or both—that is a democratic way of involving all stakeholders (i.e., teachers, classified staff, parents, board members, community members, and students). The strategic plan is a process that includes a mission, set of beliefs, goals, strategies, implementation and evaluations, or assessment of results. Regardless of the origin of a vision, it should be based on school data, facts, and student needs. Most importantly it should be clearly communicated to the school community. If supported by the school community, it provides the basis support from the community for solid moral and ethical decision making.

To determine the effectiveness of vision, an assessment of evaluative criteria needs to be developed. These assessments may include staff and community surveys, community and school demographic, socio-economic, and ethnicity information (i.e., California Basic Educational Data Systems (CBEDS), and *yes,* standardized test scores for measurement of overall student academic progress).

Shared Decision Making

Similar to a vision for moral and ethical leadership is shared decision making. In this manner, the principal or superintendent identifies a leadership team, which is composed of lower level administrators and/or teachers who are able to communicate with each other to see the "big picture" for school/district improvement. The principal finds a way to formulate a leadership team for regular and on-going communications for school improvement and other operations. There is no question that the principal or the superintendent is the ultimate decision maker at the school/district and assumes responsibility for these decisions. However, his/her shared decision making efforts generate much more support for his/her leadership and decision making that is based on local student and school community needs, than solely based on federal and state standards.

Consequences of Moral and Ethical Decision Making
There are two types of consequences for moral and ethical school leader decision making: School leaders are expected to: 1) make sound decisions regarding students and staff that exercise good and rationale judgment, and 2) consider the anticipated and real consequences for their decision making. On the first type, decisions should focus on individual cases that test both established standards, board policies and procedures, and may be made on what is most fair for the individual student or staff member, or may be made on what expectations are for the collective interest of all students. This practical decision making must consider both standards from their profession and the likely outcomes for their standards-based choices.

Philosophers, such as Immanuel Kant, refer to deontology as driving standards, policies, laws, and rules for school leader decision making. Kant introduces abstract principles in his Universal Standard in his book on Groundwork, such as The Ten Commandments, etc., to regulate daily affairs. These high-minded principles may be taken for granted, but provide leaders to think on how their actions will influence others in similar situations. Is the decision morally acceptable to the community? Is it perceived fair to the subject student or teacher and to all other students and teachers? Is it consistent? Does it conform to the mission of the school/district? How will the outcomes of the decision influence the future behavior of students and staff in the organization if a similar problem arises?

The second type of moral and ethical decision making asks school leaders to look at anticipated and real consequences for their decision making. Utilitarian philosophers fastened act and rule consequences of this approach as to whether the decision is a good one or not. In the case of a principal disciplining a child for bringing a knife as a weapon to school, act disciplinary consequences affect an individual child, while rule consequences affect all students in the entire school regarding bring a knife to school. The rule consequences will be seen as a rule for the future.

Another more complex example of consequences is the superintendent of a 10,000-student school district that has just learned that the state will deficit-fund the district approximately 10% for the following year due to a poor economy resulting in a significant shortfall of tax revenue. This revenue shortfall amounts to a huge financial hit on basic district operations. In order to balance the district budget and maintain the state mandated budget reserve, the superintendent will need to either reduce both classified and certificated staff or reduce their salaries and benefits. Both alternatives are subject to collective bargaining with the classified and certificated employees union. Yet, earlier that year, there was a provision in the newly developed strategic plan that class size will be maintained at a maximum of 28 students per class, and employee salaries and benefits will remain competitive with surrounding school districts. The class size is also consistent with regional accrediting agency requirements.

Which alternative should the superintendent recommend to the school board: 1) reduce staff salaries and benefits for all staff through furlough days, or 2) increase the class size to 30 students, resulting in the layoff of 24 teachers? Either recommendation made by this superintendent will have an enormous impact on the perceptions of fairness of his/her leadership with the teachers, parents, and community.

How District and School Images Are Influenced by School Leadership Decision Making

There is no question that a school district and school are both a space that exerts a major influence on the communities that they serve and provides a positive or negative image as to how they are perceived by their communities. Fair or not, these images include overall appearance of the school campus and grounds, student academic achievement, behavior and conduct of the students, athletic and academic competitive events and results, and overall learning environment for the students.

Much of these images are the result of educational leadership from school boards, superintendents, and deputy administrators at the district office, and school principals at the school site level. The school leadership often creates accurate perceptions among the students, teachers, staff, parents, and tax-paying community members, as reported by word-of-mouth school communications and the local press.

The perceptions that school leaders create are based on the results of their decision making practices for students, staff, and the community. All of these stakeholders hold school leaders ultimately accountable for the results of the moral and ethical nature of their decisions. They hold their school leaders in the highest esteem to be role models for the students, teachers, staff, parents, and the community. Wrong or right decisions by these leaders will shape the school and district environment toward a "good school" or a "bad school" that is not easily changed unless there is a leadership change.

Conclusion

This chapter has reviewed codes of ethics, principles, and standards as major components on school leaders exercising their decision making skills both at the district and school levels. Simultaneously, the chapter has also analyzed the moral and ethical decision making influenced by culture, backgrounds, and personal beliefs as a strong counter balance and influence on school leader decision making. School leaders have a built-in opportunity to enhance a positive district and school image because local communities generally support their district and schools, according to annual Phi Delta Kappa polls. It is their effective, professional, and creative decision making skills that will maintain this "good" school image and reputation, or create a "bad" image with the students, staff, parents, and community.

Some Things to Think About

~ How would you compare standards, principles, and codes of ethics?

~ How can standards conflict with ethical decision making? Can you provide an example?

~ How is a school's reputation and image affected by moral and ethical decision making?

~ How has the emphasis on standardized testing changed the delivery of education for all students?

References

ACSA.Org "Principles, Code of Ethics"

Fish, S. The trouble with principle. Cambridge, MA: Harvard University Press.

ISLLC (Interstate School Leaders Licensure Consortium) Standards formulated and adopted by the Chief State School Officers, usually state superintendents or commissioners (1996). California Professional Standards for Educational Leaders (CPSEL): Adopted from Interstate School Leaders Licensure Consortium (ISLLC), and adapted by California School Leadership Academy at WestEd, Association of California School Administrators, California Commission of Teacher Credentialing, California Department of Education, and various California universities and colleges.

Kant's Moral Philosophy, Stanford Encyclopedia of Philosophy, February 23, 2004; substantive revision Sunday, April 6, 2008. Retrieved from http://plato.stanford.edu/entries/kant-moral

Maxcy, S. J. (2002). Ethical school leadership. Boulder, NY: Lanham, Toronto, Plymouth, UK: Rodman & Littlefield Education.

National University, EDA 650 online course shell.

Sacks, P. Standardized minds: The high price of America's testing culture and what we can do to change it. New York: Perseus Books.

Siegel (2004) as cited in Smith, L. & Ruhl-Smith (2006). Examining ethics in educational leadership: Some basic thought for professorial analysis; AASA Journal of Scholarship and Practice (Vol. 3, No. 2). (2006, summer)

Troy, B. (2009). "Elementary school assistant principals' decision-making analyzed through four ethical frameworks of justice, critique, care, and the profession." *Theses and Dissertations* (Paper 55). Retrieved from http://scholarcommons.usf.edu/etd/55

Chapter 4

Diversity and Ethical Decision Making in the Schools

~~~~~~~~

Philosophy and moral theory suggest that making ethical decisions is a complex matter. There is no one, easy approach and it is imperative for the aspiring educational leader to develop his or her own moral compass. And this complexity and the need to understand one's moral compass are most apparent when we consider the issue of diversity; not only diversity in values, but also how those values affect our thinking regarding cultures, race, equity, religion, leadership and power, gender, and attitudes toward the disabled (to name but a few variables).

When we think of diversity, we almost always think of racial and ethnic differences. But diversity goes well beyond those differences which come to mind quickly. Culture and geography can play a significant role in our knowledge of ethical diversity, and many of the approaches to ethics we believe to be universal to all people can come into question. For example, there is the matter of cultural relativism. Vincent Ruggiero, in his chapter Comparing Cultures that is from the book *Thinking Critically About Ethical Issues* (2008), calls our attention to the Ik tribe of Central Africa. The tribe acknowledges no moral or social obligation to anyone or anything. Betrayal of neighbors is not only socially acceptable but common practice. This is borne out of the need to survive, as children are abandoned at age three and must learn to band together with others in their same predicament and fend for themselves. This hardens them and as Ruggiero points out, citing anthropologist Colin Turnbull, "when an emaciated little girl lay dying of hunger, her playmates put a bit of food in her hand and then, as she raised it to her mouth, beat her savagely. Similarly, mothers laugh when their infants fall and hurt themselves; if a leopard carries off a child, the parents' reaction is delight."

Most people in what we think of as the civilized world would find these kinds of behavior shocking and incomprehensible. It has been suggested that at one time the Ik had a more traditional sense of human behavior, but time and trial forced them to abandon that and they now live bereft of love, affection, and feeling.

While this is an extreme example, it does illustrate the point that human beings can have very different sets of ethical principles. And this raises the question for us, "Should we be judgmental about behavior and customs that are entirely alien to us but acceptable and maybe even preferable to others?" At first glance, in circumstances like this, it would appear that we should intervene and impose our ethical views on others, with that being the right thing to do. Doing so, however, might upset a survivability rhythm and/or balance in a way of life that cannot be altered.

Far less extreme (and yet very real) is dealing with different cultural mores in our own society, such as religious practices that seem quite alien to us—whether it be significant fasting and deprivation of self for protracted periods of time or attitudes about clothing, speech, or gender differences. In the late 1970s, for example, when there was an influx of Vietnamese and Hmong refugees coming to the United States, school officials noted that some children bore marks on their bodies that suggested that they had been abused. Believing this to be the case, school authorities contacted Child Protective Services and the police. This caused great alarm and concern for the parents who were often accused of abusing their children. In the end, it was discovered that these bruises were the result of folk medical treatment that left suspicious skin marks, but which in the culture was not abuse at all.

Even within the United States there is great diversity in how different people look at issues such as educational inequality, access to health care, racial profiling, and other matters (to name but a few). Viewed through political lenses and ultimately relying on often controversial Supreme Court decisions to legally—as opposed to ethically—decide the matter, there are those who believe that there is no communal responsibility to address them or to be concerned about them. Society has little or no responsibility to take care of neighbors—that is an individual responsibility. On the other hand, there are those who deeply believe that not to address these issues is socially irresponsible. Would it ever be possible that ethical decision making could be easily defined and cut and dried? In an earlier chapter of this text, we read and reflected upon the writings of different ethical philosophers from over the centuries. All of these philosophers are from the Western tradition, with much of what they say also being found in the Eastern tradition as well. They all reflected somewhat consistent but evolving perspectives on what is a common, ethical core for our world. But, as we know, not everyone in the world shares those perspectives. Do we concern ourselves with this issue or should we be open to a wide variety of ethically diverse thinking?

As future school leaders, it is necessary to always remember the social context in which we work. As interesting as cultural relativism is and as interesting as extreme cultural differences are, we come back to what is acceptable and to use Aristotle's concept of what a proper habit of virtue is. Almost all of the philosophers whom we have read and many others with whom we may be familiar suggest that it ultimately is our responsibility to promote the common social good without impinging upon appropriate individual rights of others that do not hurt either us or those we serve.

A comprehensive and most thoughtful review of ways in which school administrators can face this complexity can be found in an article in the *Journal of School Leadership* by Ulrich C. Reitzug, entitled "Diversity, Power, and Influence: Multiple Perspectives on the Ethics of School Leadership." In his article,

Reitzug describes these three perspectives for making ethical decisions:

1. Structural functionalism, which is more directed toward regulating and maintaining the prevailing and current social order, with an emphasis on rules and practices that are seen as rational, universal, and somewhat static;

2. Interpretivism, which is like structural functionalism in that it promotes the current social order but recognizes that rules cannot be universal and that the context of a given situation may require a different application of the rules; and Application of critical theory, which states that all events are value laden and, thus, has as its goal "to free organization members from sources of domination, alienation, exploitation, and repression by critiquing the existing social structure with the intent of changing it" (Gioia and Pitre, 1990, p. 588).

Utilizing these categories, Reitzug raises a number of significant questions that school administrators face as clearly today as they did in 1994 when his article was first published. What follows is an excerpt from that article.

Ethical Issues of Cultural Diversity (pp. 430–406)

Ethical issues of cultural pluralism emerge when the practices and policies of educators reflect the culture, mores, and needs of the dominant class (in school administration, white, middle-class males) and are in opposition to the culture and interests of nondominant groups. The issue is not whether individuals and groups are treated similarly or differently, but rather whether treatment results in inequitable effects. Capper (1993) argues that those holding "less political and economic power

From *Journal of School Leadership* 18 no 4 JL 2008 by Ulrich C. Reitzug. Copyright © 2008 by *Journal of School Leadership*. Reprinted by permission.

in society" (p. 5) are kept in subservient relationships to the dominant social class through what she terms invisibility/imbalance, stereotyping, and fragmentation/isolation. Specifically, invisibility/imbalance occurs in schools: (a) when administrators in predominantly white schools deny that educational disparities exist even though inequities may be present in terms of gender, social class, or some other factor (e.g., more males in math classes, more females in home economics classes); (b) through administrative denial in predominantly white schools of the importance of educating for diversity, opting instead for a curriculum that reflects local demographics (e.g., Eurocentric curriculum); (c) when schools serve a diverse group of students but curriculum and culture remain monocultural (e.g., discipline codes that reflect white, middle-class behavioral standards); (d) when practices sensitive to diversity are implemented but remain fragmented and isolated from daily school life, thus remaining "peripheral to the core instructional organization of the school" (p. 289; e.g., stand-alone events such as Black History month or Multicultural Education class); (e) when issues of diversity are central to the curriculum, but the range of people considered is narrow (e.g., students with disabilities or students with nontraditional sexual orientations are not considered); and (f) when multicultural education is inclusive and pervasive throughout the curriculum, but educational practices are not "oriented toward social reconstruction" (p. 289, e.g., minority students are disproportionally represented in discipline referrals, expulsions, etc., or are inequitably represented in gifted programs). Each of the mechanisms of invisibility/imbalance raises ethical issues for school administrators in a pluralistic society . . . . For example, in white schools where administrators deny that educational disparity exists, advising practices may be common that urge males to enroll in advanced level mathematics classes while females are more frequently referred to home economics classes. Or, students from affluent families may more heavily populate college preparatory classes, while students from poorer families make up the bulk of vocational education classes. The ethical issue for administrators and schools is the extent to which they should advocate the pursuit of educational opportunities that "feel" less comfortable to students because the opportunities are incongruent with the culturally embedded stereotypes that particular categories of students have come to accept as true (e.g., that females lack proficiency in mathematics or that working class students are better served by a curriculum that will train them for working class jobs). Such stereotyping serves to keep individuals from oppressed groups in their place. By regularly attributing certain characteristics to a group, members of that group over time come to believe in the truth of the attributes (Capper, 1993), essentially limiting their access to knowledge of other ways of being. In some instances, ethical issues of diversity may be difficult for administrators to recognize and address because ethical practice may con-flict with societal expectations of political correctness or with administrators' personal conceptions of religious values. Secondary school administrators, for example, may ignore the issue of student sexual orientation unless they are forced to address it by a critical choice situation (e.g., homosexual couple prom attendance). If we are to believe studies, however, anywhere from 1% to 10% of secondary school students are likely to be homosexual (Sears, 1993). During a period of time in their lives when all students are wrestling with their emergent sexuality, gay and lesbian students are rendered invisible when schools: (a) refuse to overtly recognize that homosexual students exist; (b) condone the mistreatment of homosexual students by refusing to hear them being called "queers," "fags," "gay-boys," "lesbos," and other derogatory terms; (c) discriminate against them via policies that legislate such things as heterosexual prom dates; and (d) fail to educate for diversity by not explicitly considering homosexuality in the curriculum.

The ethical issue for leaders is the extent of their responsibility in permitting and honoring student sexual diversity versus their responsibility to respect the sociocultural and religious values of local community members. Gender-related issues may also pose ethical dilemmas for administrators. Van Nostrand (1993) has advocated for "gender-responsible leadership" (p. xviii) and has documented administrative practices that are insensitive to gender equity. These practices may range from subtle aspects of language usage and group processes to inequitable supervision policies. Van Nostrand (1993) provides examples of leaders who allow males to dominate meetings by permitting them to participate more, interrupt women, and provide a greater number of solutions. She discusses how men knowingly or unknowingly collude in gender bias by not challenging sexist language and practices and how women collude by adhering to socially constructed gender expectations. Supervision policies may treat males and females the same and thus not recognize gender differences in responsiveness to supervisory practice, or they may treat males and females differentially but in inequitable ways (Shakeshaft, 1993). What responsibility do leaders have for challenging overt sexism? Does responsibility extend to challenging subtler aspects of sexism that may be unknowingly perpetrated by others? What is the leader's responsibility for facilitating the education of staff members in terms of gender-responsible leadership and gender-responsible teaching? Examining ethical criteria suggested by structural functionalism, interpretivism, and critical theory may help us address ethical issues such as these.

Another way to look at determining our awareness of diversity and ethics in the schools is to examine our own sensitivity to it. Monte Salyer (1990) has developed a six-stage model—almost suggesting the Kubler-Ross stages of grief model—that proposes a progression of awareness that can be used as a scale to determine where we personally are regarding our individual understanding of diversity. The model's stages are

1. Ignorance—being somewhat uninformed and imperceptive of their being any multicultural diversity in a given context, even when it is obvious;

2. Rejection—avoiding any diverse situation or, if confronted with it, resorting to negative stereotyping or even segregation of those who are different;

3. Approximation—the "it's a small world" view that allows us to accept others as ourselves but in different costumes—a view that does not want to accept that there really are those with values significantly different from our own;

4. Awareness—cognitively accepting that there is cultural diversity, including values, in our leadership context, but not yet appreciating those differences;

5. Approval—recognizing diversity and accepting it, and as the term says, actually approving of this diversity and affirming it; and

6. Versatility—being able to live comfortably and respectfully with different cultures, perhaps best typified in successful bi-cultural marriages, with understanding and perhaps most importantly, being empathetic with other cultures.

Salyer invites us to consider these six stages of cultural sensitivity, to rate ourselves as to where we are, and to ponder how this knowledge can make us better educators. While he writes primarily from a teacher's perspective, the stages he presents are equally important for school leaders to consider.

Some Things to Think About

~ What is your thinking about cultural relativism? Should it play a role in setting your ethical compass as a school leader?

~ Reitzug raises a number of questions about diversity that school leaders must confront. How would you respond to the questions he raises? What should a school leader do when confronted with those kinds of questions?

~ Salyer offers us a six-stage rating scale to assess where we are personally regarding diversity. How would you rate yourself and do you think that this scale provides us with a valid analysis?

~ Some ethical philosophers, such as Rawls whom we discussed in Chapter 2, call upon us to consider social justice in making ethical decisions. Should we do that, especially in matters concerning diversity?

~ Consider the following cases and tell us what you think should be done.

1. Dr. Countem is the controller for the district. His role includes keeping track of the budgets for the schools in a district with a mixture of schools with affluent and poor families. For the most part, the children of the affluent parents attend new schools in the newer section of the school district. Children of less affluent parents attend schools in need of repair and lacking current instructional equipment. Dr. Countem has been given the charge by the Board to allocate funds for school updating. Parents of the affluent children have lobbied hard (while noting that they are colleagues of community leaders) that it is important to have showcase schools with the latest in computer technology that would attract clean industry to the district and be an economic boon to residents of the district. Consequently, they think it best that the majority of the limited funds available should go to the schools that their children attend as it would help the community prosper. On the other hand, there is the argument (for which there are no vocal advocates) that equity calls for putting

the majority of the funds into improving the schools attended by the children of the poorer parents. Dr. Countem needs to be careful in his report to the Board.

2. Mr. Thrashem, vice-principal at the local middle school with an ethnically and socio-economically diverse student body, is responsible for discipline. From his experience, he has concluded that children from lower social-economic backgrounds and from minority groups tend to have a higher rate of discipline referrals than other students. Some have questioned why this is so and Mr. Thrashem says it is just the way it is and that the only way to deal with it is to be especially "tough" on this group so that they will be better disciplined when they are older. He calls it his brand of "tough love" and does not think the other students need it.

3. Ms. Ambivalence, the new high school assistant principal for discipline, has just heard a student rumor that a freshman boy has been bullied by others in his physical education class. The boy is quiet, not particularly athletic, of small build, and he has longer hair. He is accused of being gay and it was reported that he was taunted with anti-gay epithets. He, in fact, may be gay, but Ms. Ambivalence does not know that to be the case. She goes to the boy's physical education teacher, Coach Blocker, who says he has not heard of the bullying and he would not allow such a thing to happen in any event. And, he observes, boys will be boys and they need to be able to take that kind of teasing—it is all a part of toughening up and growing up. Since this is a very conservative school community and no one would like to suggest that there could be anti-gay bullying, Ms. Ambivalence is afraid to act. She may just let things go on and see what happens.

References

Capper, C. A. (1993). Educational administration in a pluralistic society. Albany, NY: State University of New York Press.

Gioia, D. A. & Pitre, E. (1990). "Multiparadigm Perspectives on Theory Building." *Academy of Management Review, 15*(4):584–602.

Reitzug, U. C. (1992, October). "Ethical Issues Confronting School Leaders in a Pluralistic Society: Implications from Multiple Paradigms." Paper presented at the University Council for Educational Administration Conference, Minneapolis, MN.

Reitzug, U. (1933). "Diversity, Power and Influence: Multiple Perspectives on the Ethics of School Leadership." *Journal of School Leadership* (Vol. 18, No. 4, July 2008).

Ruggerio, V. (2008). Thinking Critically about Ethical Issues. New York: McGraw-Hill.

Salyer, M. (1993). "Educators and Cultural Diversity: A Six-Stage Model of Cultural Versatility." *Education* (Vol. 113, Issue 3, Spring 1993).

Sears, J. T. (1993). "Responding to the Sexual Diversity of Faculty and Students: Sexual Praxis and the Critically Reflective Administrator." In Educational Administration in a Pluralistic Society, C. A. Capper (Ed.). Albany, NY: State University of New York Press (pp. 110–172).

Shakeshaft, C. (1993). "Gender Equity in Schools." In Educational Administration in a Pluralistic Society, C. A. Capper (Ed.). Albany, NY: State University of New York Press (pp. 86–109).

Van Nostrand, C. H. (1993). Gender-Responsible Leadership: Detecting Bias, Implementing Interventions. Newbury Park, CA: Sage.

Wynne, E. A. (1989). "Managing Effective Schools: The Moral Element." In Educational Policy for Effective Schools, K. A.

Chapter 5

School Leadership and Ethics from a Woman's Perspective

"... strong women can make both men and women feel uncomfortable. Their style challenges feminine norms, in particular, women's leadership. This strength, if not exercised properly, can create discomfort and distance with school board members, school district staff, and the community. The words "aggressive" and "bitchy" have been used to describe "strong women."

Dana and Bourisaw (2006, p. 123)

This rather profound comment foreshadows a discussion of ethics, women, and educational leadership in this chapter. I trust no one is offended by the description of women given here or the epithet they are called too often. It seems *de rigueur* to call any woman who exercises her authority in a strong and confident manner by this name, yet we have nothing quite so harsh, so frequently used, or so egregiously misplaced, when referring to the male gender who perform the same actions.

As the only female author of this text, I have chosen to take a rather strong position on women as leaders. My co-authors have been encouraging and supportive, yet I must acknowledge they do not always share my sentiments. I suspect many of you will not, but if the controversy over my research ignites more conversation on the topic, then I will feel that I have fulfilled my responsibility. As we explore gender differences in educational leadership, I would hope that my chapter will bring thought provoking comments and, ultimately, add value to your practice.

Barbara J. Salice, Ed.D
San Diego, California

Any literature that can be found on gender differences in education leadership positions appears to be slim and suggests that women need to "fit into" the male model. Over the last two decades, while there have been significant advances for women in educational leadership positions, there still exists a disproportionate difference between the genders, suggesting that women have not "fit" the male leadership model. Quoting from Polka & Litchka (2008) in their book *The Dark Side of Educational Leadership*:

> In 2000, there were 13,728 school superintendents across America with 1,984 women superintendents (14.4 percent), and according to the American Association of School Administrators (2007), as of 2006, approximately 78.3% superintendents were men, while 21.7% were women (pp. 65–66).

While there were gains, they were small. In just six years, only 7.3% more women joined the ranks of educational superintendents. Numerous studies indicate ". . . that women are rated as well or higher than their male counterparts in a range of leadership abilities, skills, and competencies" (Kouzes & Posner, 2002), yet they are not obtaining the more advanced leadership roles for which they have been educated and vetted. Why the paradox? We will be able to address this issue when we examine some of the philosophy that drives women's ethics and distinguishes it from male ethics. Perhaps, we will find that there is a common sense reason for the disparity in women's educational leaders, and perhaps we will find a solution that approaches or, at least, suggests ways in which women can be successful at their jobs, without being feared, distant and, yes, bitchy.

In taking on this assignment to write a chapter on women, ethics, and educational leadership, I was convinced that times had changed since "my day." Back in the 60s, when I started teaching, all the teachers were women and the principal was always a male. I didn't even question this hierarchy, as it appeared no woman was capable of being a principal. At that time, you either became a teacher or a nurse and you did not aspire to anything greater, especially any position that precluded more time away from home and the family.

Things have changed dramatically in the past 50 years, both for women and men, but the one feature of education that has not changed is the element of caring that pervades this profession. Albeit both education and nursing are "caring" professions by definition, women, in particular, have been the purveyors of a philosophy of caring based on natural law and feminine orientation, since the beginning of time. Male orientation to caring, in most cases, has to be learned, as men are brought up differently and influenced greatly by other male models in the family. The question of "nature" or "nurture" bears consideration, however, as this is not entirely true of all males and especially not of all cultures. Nevertheless, in educational administration caring combined with a strong sense of duty and responsibility can present challenges and opportunities to all administrators, but specifically women administrators.

No one says this better than Nel Noddings in her classic work *Caring: A Feminine Approach to Ethics and Moral Education* (1984). Ms. Noddings examines caring as a feminine phenomenon and further extends the discussion to explore a view of ethics that is significantly different than men's. She devotes a great many pages to what it means to care and be cared for, how caring for another person relates to the larger moral picture, and how caring ultimately functions in an educational context. Noddings' book is a classic and should be read by both men and women in educational leadership positions. Having searched the literature for specific differences on how women and men "care," I found there is little current research on this topic that might address the educational leaders of the 21st century. My response is: why?

First, let's look at the philosophical foundations for ethics and reflect on any similarities or differences between men and women. In his book *Ethics of Educational Leadership* (2001), Ronald Rebore states:

> *"Ethics is concerned with human conduct, as distinguished from mere human behavior. Conduct implies that there is a choice; people can choose one course of action or an alternative course of action. Behavior is a descriptive term referring to all human activities. People can behave in a rational or irrational manner. The underlying assumption is that conduct is rational because it is intentional."*

Using this definition, it would appear there are no differences between the genders on ethics. Both men and women conduct themselves in a rational manner with good intentions always as the focus of their deeds. In reality, however, we are aware that several leaders, in all areas of life, do not conduct themselves in an ethical manner. In the first chapter, numerous examples were highlighted of egregious moral behavior on the part of several individuals, all men, who were dishonest and deceptive to an unfathomable degree. No mention was made of women, however, and if history serves us well, very few women are included among the Skilling's, Lay's, or Madoff's. There was Martha Stewart, but her crime (insider trading) seemed like child's play compared to Enron, WorldCom, Tyco, AIG, and of course, the Bernard Madoff investment scandal.

Let us not forget that Martha Stewart served a year for her offense, but former Governor Eliot Spitzer was rewarded with a show on CNN for his involvement in prostitution.

This leads us to the question: Is there a difference in ethical decision making between men and women? Does gender play a role in moral reasoning and judgment and, if so, how does this impact educational practice? And most notably, do words match actions? Spitzer is an excellent example of a crime-fighting governor who participated in the very crime that he was prosecuting.

In the movie "The Whistleblower" (2010), Kathryn Bolkovac is the only woman on the UN Peacekeeping Force in Bosnia. She witnessed crimes being committed, women being abused, and corruption that was as far reaching as the UN high command. Yet, not one male would take action. Only she felt a sense of duty and responsibility to put an end to the horrific practices being imposed on women in Bosnia. Ms. Bolkovac, played by Rachel Weisz, demonstrated her capacity to be receptive and responsive to these women, who were being sold into sexual slavery. The men did not seem to "care" and chided her for her humanitarian efforts.

This theme plays out in several other movies, notably "Erin Brockovich" (2000), "The Contender" (2000), etc., and the stories of other notable women who were "whistleblowers" including Rosa Parks, Lt. General Claudia J. Kennedy, and the women who exposed Enron: Watkins, Cooper and Rowley. Often, the stakes are high for women "whistleblowers." They are fired, blacklisted, sexually harassed, and branded as troublemakers. They find too often that there is a double standard where morals and ethics are involved, and the "male" model is the one most often followed.

The implication, therefore, that I am making is that an all-male club protects itself, makes a conscious decision to do nothing, and in many ways, actually impedes a solution. This is not to say ALL men act this way, but with the numerous corporate, religious, government, and school scandals, most of, if not all the main culprits have been men. Women, however, do not have a "club." They act independently, often with courage, compassion, and commitment to do the "right thing." Women, it would appear, have a stronger ethical compass and this may, in fact, eliminate them from ever joining the "club." As I alluded to in the beginning of this chapter, women must learn to "fit in."

Men have defined the culture for so long that it is unfathomable that it will change, simply because more women are on corporate and school boards, government, or industry. Will women, however, be able to influence more men due to their feminine approach to morality and ethics? As Grimshaw (1986) points out ". . . this difference is rooted in a differing psychic development" (p. 187). Indeed, Grimshaw does invoke shades of Freud and his sexist views, especially on emotions, but they should not be dismissed, as history has proven women to do more caretaking and have a more caregiving nature than men. Carol Gilligan's *In a Different Voice* (1984) further extends the research on Freud's gender socialization theory and suggests that ". . . as adults the sexes will bring different ethical values to their work roles, differentially shaping their work-related decisions."

Gilligan elaborates on this concept by establishing her own theory of women's moral development, which has some relevance to Kohlberg's mentioned earlier in the book. The distinct differences lay in Kohlberg's orientation that focused mainly on males and placed females on a lower scale of moral development. Basically, once again, we describe women's perceptions of caring and responsibility to others as their moral foundation. Gilligan suggests that women progress through three distinct levels and two transition periods, with each representing a more sophisticated understanding of self and responsibility.

> At level one of Gilligan's theoretical framework a woman's orientation is towards individual survival (Belknap, 2000); the self is the sole object of concern. The first transition that takes place is from being selfish to being responsible. At level two the main concern is that goodness is equated with self-sacrifice (Belknap, 2000). This level is where a woman adopts societal values and social membership. Gilligan refers to the second transition from level two to level three as the transition from goodness to truth (Belknap, 2000). Here, the needs of the self must be deliberately uncovered, as they are uncovered the woman begins to consider the consequences of the self and other (Belknap, 2000).

My research led me to want to interview past, current, and future women administrators, and seek to discover the following: a. Were their ethics any different than the men with whom they worked? b. Had they encountered an ethical dilemma in their practice? c. What are good ethical and moral practices for women in educational administration?

Eileen (65), Jan (54), and Olivia (38) have had a total of almost 60 years in the teaching profession. Eileen was an assistant principal at a city middle school for ten years; Jan currently serves as the learning specialist for a school district; and Olivia is a teacher/coordinator for the AVID program (Advanced Via Individualized Determination). Each was interviewed separately and provided a wealth of information about their past or current positions, as well as expressing the joy and satisfaction they have experienced in the profession. Eileen, in particular, had numerous examples of issues that challenged her professional and personal ethics including: criminal activities at the school site, sexual abuse cases, and suicide. As vice-principal she was responsible for discipline and safe conduct on the campus. She was guided by both the school education code and the law, but most significantly by her conscience that directed her to do what was "right" and "just" for the safety of the students. In many ways, Eileen had the stark reality of dealing with everyday issues that arise in an urban middle school, most notably students bringing weapons to campus. Adherence to public law was most prominent and knowledge of referring agencies was important in every situation she encountered.

Jan had been a principal of a small grade school before being moved to the district office. Ethical and moral issues were minimal at this school site. When moving to the district office, however, although she has not recognized any ethical issues among her colleagues, she did recognize a difference in style among her supervisors, especially those that came from an ethnic background different than hers. Jan's immediate supervisor (a woman) took on a strong, controlling persona that at times makes it difficult for her to engage in conversation and discussion about important administrative matters. Jan advised that a "fit" is necessary in order for an individual to perform their roles successfully as an administrator at the district level. She believes the "glass ceiling" has been broken and that it does not matter whether or not a man or a woman is hired for an administrative position, but rather that their education, skills, and talent match the criteria for the job. In my interview, Jan noted that in this particular district a woman has never been hired as superintendent.

For several years, Olivia has entertained the thought of a high-level administrative position. She was awarded her Masters in Educational Leadership and coordinates a program especially designed for average students who show promise of succeeding in college, if given the proper encouragement, support, and resources. Olivia has enjoyed this experience so well that she has decided she does not want to be an administrator. While still working in the school district, she prefers to stay in the classroom and coordinate the AVID program, until that time when she may use it as a segue to the corporate world. She has not experienced any ethical issues and her "style" has added value to the program, as she exudes a great sense of caring for the students and her colleagues. Her reasons for no longer pursuing an administrative position revolve around her sense of dedication to the AVID program and its students, her family, and her maternal instincts to want to nurture these middle school students.

In all three interviews, it was evident that these women were equipped to handle any ethical situation that presented itself, given their background and training to be an administrator and knowledge of school, district, and state codes. All three demonstrated a great amount of caring and concern for their students, as not seen as often in men and in keeping with the general consensus suggested by Nel Noddings (1984) that there are deep "psychological structures that may be responsible for this mode of caring" (p. 40). While training for both sexes may be similar, it appears that the genetic makeup is different or "something else" for women.

All three interviewees adhere to school and district codes, when applicable, yet their sense of relationship, caring, and compassion were strongly evident. Only Eileen appeared to encounter serious moral issues. Yet, Jan and Olivia had a strong commitment to being ethical both personally and professionally. Most significantly, all three felt the need "to do the right thing" when conflict arose. Furthermore, the information gleaned from these interviews suggested that leadership style is very important and that a strong ethical model is required, if one is to be a successful educational administrator.

This brings us to a discussion of how women "fit" the male role model. As mentioned earlier in her book *In a Different Voice* (1984), Ms. Gilligan suggests that men and women differ in how they approach moral dilemmas. "Men" she contends "are likely to consider moral issues in terms of justice, rules, and individual rights. Women, on the other hand, tend to consider such issues in terms of relationship, caring, and compassion." When confronted with a moral conflict, the research validates that women look beyond the issue of justice, rules, etc., and attempt to see the bigger picture that involves feelings, attitudes, and perceptions, even interpretations. Women, it would appear, are more sensitive to moral issues and look at the big picture and the affect their decision will have on their school and community. This is not to imply ALL women act this way, but there is a definite distinction in how a male principal would handle a similar situation. His approach would be more structured, following the rules (to the letter of the law), and reducing the situation to a minimalist perspective.

We have already established that the "all male club" does exist, that to some extent the "glass ceiling" has been cracked, but there are still restrictions and nuances that keep women from joining "the club." In their book *The Dark Side of Educational Leadership* (2008), the authors Polka & Litchka make the point that when women superintendents in their study were viewed as traditionally "female," their strengths and weaknesses were perceived differently than those of males. Furthermore, when women superintendents behaved in a manner that was consistent with traditional male forms of leadership behavior, they were perceived as being less effective as a superintendent (p. 78). This, indeed, leaves us with a conundrum. How is a woman to act in a leadership position? If she is too "male" oriented, she is often called the "b" word; if she acts too feminine, she is looked upon as being weak, inefficient, or unproductive.

Is there a middle road or should women begin to create their own "club" to better address the gender differences that exist in leadership positions? Furthermore, do women possess a different set of ethical skills than men and are these skills and dispositions impeding their progress to higher levels of educational administration? Are we able to conclusively and definitively answer this question? The simple response is "no." Why? Because we are all human beings and we are all operating from different backgrounds, cultures, mores, and values. We would trust that there are underlying assumptions that are grounded in rational and correct behavior that is intent on always doing the "right thing."

What are some of those "right" things? This is difficult to say, as what is "right" in one situation may be compromised or altered in another. Take for example, the following true story of a high school counselor at an all girls' Catholic school. The first this institution ever hired. The counselor was expected to perform academic and career counseling, not clinical or personal counseling. Yet the young women who attended this very conservative, rigidly structured institution found the new young counselor the only person who would listen to their concerns. Nuns who came from a very strict religious orientation operated the school. Even in the 80s, they refused to move from habits to street clothes. The principal was a woman who provoked fear in everyone with whom she worked.

On one occasion, a young woman in her junior year approached the counselor not with academic or career issues, but issues of sexual abuse. She told the counselor that her father had been abusing her for years, but now that she was getting older, he was replacing her with her younger sister who was 12. This was the 80s and this particular behavior was not as public, as it is today. The counselor immediately brought the situation to the principal, who instructed her to "forget about it." The father is a "big supporter" of the school and makes generous donations. The counselor was shocked, but since this was a private, Catholic school and no public regulations regarding child abuse were in place at this time, she could do nothing. The principal was the ultimate authority. Much to the counselor's chagrin, she was fired a few weeks later.

This situation provokes thoughts of the Joe Paterno situation at Penn State as mentioned previously in chapter one. In both the Paterno and the counselor's cases, each failed to directly intervene and take action to prevent the abuse. In both cases, they notified higher authorities that chose to ignore the situation, or as Dr. Hoban identified, they exercised "benign neglect." Should Paterno and the counselor have gone above their superiors? If they did, what would have been the consequences? Indeed, in each case both parties were fired. In the counselor's case, she was stymied and intimidated by the principal. Furthermore, the counselor had been brought up to respect authority and at this school, the principal was the ultimate authority. Both personally and religiously, the counselor did not know what to do next, as the principal's dictum was law. In Paterno's case, he felt he had passed the issue on to higher authorities and that it was now their issue to move it forward.

It is important that we look at this issue in a historical perspective. In the 80s, we were not as informed about abuses, especially those in the Catholic Church. More and more incidents of child and sexual abuse have become common. Furthermore, laws, rules, and regulations have been enacted that address these issues. Today, the school counselor, teacher, and administrative staff would have no excuse for not reporting such an incident to the police or child welfare services. Options such as these did not exist at that time, or if they did, they were vague, ambiguous, and most notably, ignored.

The point I'm trying to make is that both Joe Pa and the counselor strove to do "the right thing." I felt the counselor did as much of the "right" thing as humanely possible, given the leadership issues and climate of the school. She did the "right" thing and lost her job. The same situation applied to Joe Paterno. Perhaps, in hindsight, both Paterno and the counselor should have done more (i.e., called higher authorities, continued to counsel the young woman or man, etc.). We may never know Paterno's rationalization for not doing more. We know the counselor was stopped dead in her efforts by an "old school" mentality that put the finances of the school far ahead of the safety of a young woman.

In closing, I would like to highlight the following thoughts:

1. Ethics should NOT be gender specific, albeit I have demonstrated that it is through various authors and research. We need to make ethics universal. We need to follow Immanuel Kant's philosophy of just "doing the right thing" without any caveats.

2. Duty is at the heart of our profession. Every teacher and administrator must pledge themselves to do their best for our children, community, and country. We must remain competent, committed, and enthusiastic about our work.

3. The "old" paradigms no longer "fit" today's educational administrators. With the plethora of rules and regulations, and oversight and accountability measures, it is difficult to almost impossible to make an unethical decision. Yet, many will. They have lost their moral compass and are attracted by greed, power, and position. They have lost their sense of duty.

4. The male "club" is alive and well and it is difficult, if not impossible, to navigate these waters. What is required is a deep and thorough understanding of the culture that male administrators embrace. As stated earlier, men see their leadership roles in terms of justice, rules, and individual rights. Women do not necessarily see it this way. While men continue to dominate and define the field, however, women will have to educate themselves to these gender persuasions, and at the same time, attempt to influence the male leaders to adopt more female orientations, such as caring and compassion. Let me be quite clear, however, that my analysis is generalized and that there are many caring and compassionate male administrators in our school systems, but there are not enough of them.

What will it take for a woman administrator to be credible and respected by their male colleagues? What will it take to change the numbers, so that we see more females in more superintendencies and other leadership positions at the state and national level?

My simple answer to this is "gravitas"—that certain something that sets an individual apart from others. Pundits, such as Bill O'Reilly, suggested that Katie Couric of ABC news did not have her contract renewed because she lacked "gravitas." Walter Cronkite, Peter Jennings, and Edward R. Morrow did. Admittedly, Couric has currently been rehired by NBC to launch another show. It does not, however, require the same "gravitas" that ABC news required. It is a "talk show," where I am sure Ms. Couric will do well. She has personality. She has charisma. She is the "all-American gal" who personifies intelligence, security, sensitivity, sex appeal, and style. But does she have "gravitas"? Does she reflect leadership ability? Does she project and demand "respect"?

Indeed, if we were to make a comparison between her and Brian Williams, I suspect we'd see a significant difference. This is the point I am trying to make when we compare male and female differences in ethical decision making. While men do not have to prove they have "gravitas," women still do. Women are still not taken seriously when it comes to making major decisions of importance or significance. There is always a caveat to their promulgations (i.e., she was tired, she was stressed, and she suffers from female problems, family comes first, etc.) ad nauseam. You would almost never hear such rationale applied to male counterparts.

In her book *The Princessa: Machiavelli for Women* (1997), Harriet Rubin appears to be addressing the concept of "gravitas," when she suggests ways in which women can get what they want. She encourages us ". . . to learn the means by which you can get what you want. Not by assertiveness or aggression. Not by raising your voice, or a fist; not by brutal means, but by becoming a presence of great authority" (p. 5).

The Princessa is a great classic that spins off the original classic *The Prince*. All women should read it. In Rubin's book, the "princessa" is a woman unlike all other women. She is strong, ethical, and uncompromising, and she is very much aware that women and men are NOT equal. She uses this concept, however, to positively reinforce the fact that women have strengths and possibilities that men do not possess. She believes women's strengths live in the "subtle weapons" that are hers alone. Although some fifteen years old, the author is alluding to just those features of women's gifts in ethical decision-making that have been mentioned earlier: care, sensitivity, and relationships. Furthermore, she encourages women to NOT play by the rules of the game (i.e., don't join the men's club).

A major portion of the book focuses on power: how women should get it and how they can retain it. It is not my intent to explore this concept further, as I feel I have addressed it in perhaps a subtler manner and I would like to return to the importance of gravitas. I would, however, encourage all of you—men and women—to read this very profound work.

At this time in our educational system, we need both men and women who have "gravitas." The times call for leaders of great ability. Never before have administrators been faced with such serious issues as bullying, intimidation, suicides, and killings on campus as they do today. At this time, in this era, we need administrators who reflect major commitment to their duty and the responsibilities inherent in being an administrator in the K–12 setting. We need those people, male and female, who have "gravitas."

Some Things to Think About

~ How did you react emotionally to the information in this chapter?

~ In what ways will the information impact your practice?

~ Can you identify an ethical dilemma where there were no-ticeable differences in the way a male or female leader handled an ethical dilemma?

~ How would you assess Kohlberg's theory of moral develop-ment with Gilligan's? Are there major distinctions between the sexes in their moral development?

~ Now that we have discussed the classic words of feminism and ethics by Noddings (1984), Gilligan (1984), and Rubin (1997), can you determine its relevancy to the challenges women face today in educational administration?

~ Do you accept the concept of "gravitas," as a pivotal issue in getting women what they want? Why do women still have to prove they have "gravitas"?

~ What three questions would you ask the author of this chapter, given the opportunity to communicate with her?

References

Belknap, R. A. (2000). One woman's life viewed through the interpretive lens of Gilligan's theory. *Violence Against Women, 6,* 586–605.

Dana, J. A., & Bourisan, D. M. (2006). *Women in the superintendency: Discarded leadership.* Lanham, MD: Rowen & Littlefield.

DeVito, D. (Producer) & Sodenbergh, S. (Director) (2000). "Erin Brockovich." United States: Universal Pictures.

Gilligan, C. (1984). *In a different voice: Psychological theory and women's development.* Cambridge, MA: Harvard University Press.

Grimshaw, J. (1986). Philosophy and feminist thinking. Cambridge, MA: Harvard University Press.

Kouzes, J., & Posner, B. (2002) as stated in Polka, W. & Litchka, P. (2008). *The dark side of educational leadership.* Lanham, MD: Rowan and Littlefield.

Kaufman, A., Rattratm, C., & Pioresan, C. (Producers) & Kondracki, L. (Director) (2010). "The Whistleblower." Denmark: Samuel Goldwyn Films.

Oldman, G., & Urbanski, D. (Producers) & Lurie, R. (Director) (2000). "The Contender." United States: DreamWorks Pictures.

Mertz, N. T. (Ed.). (2009). *Breaking into the all male club.* Albany, NY: State University of New York Press.

Noddings, N. (1984). *Caring: A feminine approach to ethics and moral education.* Berkeley & Los Angeles, CA: University of California Press.

Polka, W., & Litchka, P. (Eds.). (2008). *The dark side of educational leadership.* Lanham, MD: Rowan & Littlefield.

Rebore, R. W. (2001). Ethics of educational leadership. Upper Saddle River, NJ: Prentice-Hall, Inc.

Rubin, H. (1997). *The princessa: Machiavelli for women.* New York: Doubleday.

Chapter 6

The Real World of Ethical Problems and School Leadership: Case Studies

In the previous five chapters, we have discussed ethics and school leadership from a variety of perspectives. We have raised the question of why we, as future school leaders, should study ethics and how we need to set our own personal and ethical compasses to guide us in our everyday actions. We have read selections from ethical philosophers from over the ages. We have noted that there is often a difference between ethics in the abstract and the codes and standards of ethics they both inspire and propose for school leaders. And we have not hesitated to consider more complex matters such as diversity and ethics and their interaction in school leadership, or to present what some might think is a controversial look at the possibility that women school leaders might see ethics in the schools from a very different perspective than men. In the end, however, it is not the abstract perspectives or theories that count. It is the real world application of what we know, believe, and are ready to act upon that is so important.

In this chapter, we shall consider the application of what we have discussed in previous chapters by focusing on ethical challenges school leaders can face in several different areas—business and school finance, school law, curriculum, communicating with parents and students, personnel matters, athletics, and the always eye brow raising topics of sex, politics, and religion. We shall approach each of these topics with a brief introduction followed by the presentation of some case studies to analyze. The case studies are based upon actual situations experienced by the authors of this book or situations inspired by cases reported by the news media.

Business and School Finance

While ethical behavior is expected of people in public life working with customers and clients, there have been notable exceptions such as politicians, new and used automobile dealerships, sports figures, and celebrities. However, in recent years, executives and senior management officials in major corporations have also been added to the list of unethical behavior, which has been previously discussed in this book. Examples include Bernie Madoff and his Ponzie scheme, Enron, WorldCom (renamed MCI, then later acquired by Verizon), etc., which have shocked and eroded the confidence and trust of company stockholders and the general public. In mid 2012, JPMorgan Chase chief executive officer, Jamie Dimon, reported a $2 billion loss with the bank from high-risk investments, which shocked world finance markets. Not much earlier, Wal-Mart's image was tarnished when The New York Times alleged bribery was a big factor in its rapid growth in Mexico.

Although public sector business officials (i.e., chief school business officers, city, county, and state business executives) have generally been held to a higher standard of ethics than comparable private executives, the general public has demanded more accountability in scrutinizing expenditures and the use of taxpayer funds to improve student academic performance. As previously mentioned, No Child Left Behind legislation has placed enormous pressure on school districts to show effective results of the expenditure of taxpayer funds. The public has become much less tolerant of wasting public funds in circumstances such as school and local official contract buyouts for either poor job performance or lack of work compatibility with governing boards or city councils. As an example, the city council of a small central coast California town paid $230,000 out of the city's dwindling budget reserves for a buyout settlement with the city's female chief of police over allegations of sexual harassment of her police officers and illegal traffic ticket quotas (San Luis Obispo Tribune, 2012).

It is common knowledge that chief school business officers are in charge of huge sums of public funds and have a fiduciary responsibility over these funds. This involves developing and presenting a budget to the governing board, collecting district revenues, monitoring expenditures, and providing accurate reports to the board, county office of education, and the state department of education regarding the fiscal health of the school district. Beyond revenues and expenditures, school business officials are responsible for all assets and operations belonging to the school district (i.e., multi-million dollar school plants and facilities, food service operations, and maintenance) that have a direct impact on the quality of education for its young people.

Public education is big business in every community in economic terms, meaning that it is a large market for servicing by multiple vendors who provide goods and services for local school districts. At state and national conventions, these vendors compete with each other to display their goods and services. Not only do school business officials interact with a variety of vendors, they also interact with superintendents, principals, and other school administrators and offer them opportunities for illegal and unethical interactions with vendors as incentives to purchase their goods and services. Although such behavior rarely occurs, school administrators and subordinates are responsible for maintaining the highest standards. These responsibilities are particularly important since school business officials have unique and intricate responsibilities (i.e., budget code intricacies, long-term debt refinancing, and purchasing from bids, etc.) that are more difficult for observation and scrutiny from other educators. Chief school business officials' ethical practices set the tone for creating or preventing abuses.

Some Cases to Ponder

Case #1:

As a middle school principal, you are a delegator. School finance is not your area of expertise. A quiet report is brought to you that your activities director has been siphoning off money to run a project for homeless students. You know the students who allegedly benefit from this. If you take action, they will be in dire straits. Also, you do not have hard evidence that anything wrong has been done. It is all hearsay.

1. What steps would you take to investigate this quiet report?

2. How would you determine the source of revenue to run a project for homeless students?

3. Whom would you alert about these allegations?

4. What action would you take if there was truth to this quiet report?

Case #2:

You are the chief school business official and have prided yourself in being fiscally conservative and above all in keeping careful track of all expenditures. You have recently discovered that your boss, the superintendent, has been requesting additional compensation for unused vacation time instead of taking entitled vacation days off. He has not informed the board of the additional compensation in lieu of vacation days and there is nothing in either the open or closed board meeting minutes. You are concerned that this will become an audit exception next June.

1. Should you confront your boss, the superintendent, about his problem?

2. If the superintendent becomes defensive, should you inform the board and risk losing your job as chief business officer?

3. Should you inform the county office of education chief business officer who provides oversight of local district budgets?

4. What will you say to the auditor who finds an audit exception of this practice?

———

Case #3:

As the superintendent, you have been involved in a major new building construction program in your district, and have working closely with the architect to put together a set of specifications to put the project out to bid. The school board has approved the specifications and advertising for bids. After one month, you receive four bids and are surprised that your board president, who is a general contractor, has put in a bid. At the bid opening meeting, you are further surprised to learn that he has submitted the lowest bid. There is a board policy on conflict of interest that may preclude a board president from getting the low bid. Another bidder who was the second to the lowest bidder has already threatened to sue the school board and district if the board accepts the low bid from the board president.

1. How should you handle this situation with the board president and the remaining board members?

2. What kind of legal advice should you seek from the school district attorney?

3. Should you recommend that the board accept the lowest bid even though it's from the board president?

4. What would you say to the other bidders? To the press?

———

School Law

In earlier chapters, we have mentioned that while it is an ideal situation when school law and ethical decision making act in harmony, more often than not that is not the case. Real life is more complex than that. School law is most often specific and it provides clear directions, especially in states like California, where the education code makes it very clear as to what school administrators shall do (are mandated to do) or may do (it is optional).

Being a school leader is a human enterprise and it is the human part of things that often, perhaps most often, influences how we as school leaders apply the law and make ethical decisions. Some of the factors that can influence us are our knowledge of the law, our relationship with our peers and our students, and the pressure we can get from the community. Throughout this book, we have referred to one's ethical compass—that inner set of moral/ethical directions that guide us when we make decisions. That compass is set by so many factors as we have observed: our knowledge of the law, our religious and personal values, our own cultural values as opposed to those of our students and parents which might be different, and maybe even a gender bias of which we might not even be aware.

Another variable we have not considered, although it is implied in our consideration of our personal values, is our sense of fairness, justice, and our empathy and compassion. Arguably, school leaders (most of who come from the ranks of teachers) are sensitive and caring individuals. Education is a helping profession, and compassion and empathy are among its hallmarks. So, too, are our sense of justice—the letter of the law and fairness. When we consider fairness, we think about how strictly we must apply the letter of the law while balancing that with any mitigating factors that should come into play. And then, even if we do that and find that we should act as enforcers of strict justice, should we also show mercy? This dilemma is illustrated many times in literature, but perhaps most saliently in the references which follow.

In William Shakespeare's *The Merchant of Venice*, Portia makes the case for compassion when she states:

> *The quality of mercy is not strain'd, It droppeth as the gentle rain from Heaven Upon the place beneath; it is twice blest; It blesses him that giveth and him that takes; Act IV (c 1597)*

John Milton, in Paradise Lost, has God say of the fallen: "I shall temper justice with mercy." Chapter X (1667) Posing the opposite view, however, is the thought of Edward Young who writes in his Night Thoughts (1742), "A God all mercy is a God unjust." There are those whose ethical compass is more drawn toward mercy, and those whose compass is more drawn toward strict justice.

How much can we "bend the rules" and how rigid should we be? Education, almost by its very nature as we have noted, attracts caring people although the literature is complete with opposite types such as Charles Dickens' Mr. M'Choakumchild in Bleak House. But once one becomes a school administrator, there can be pressure to significantly curb one's propensity to be a caring individual, especially if one is a caring person and begins service as an assistant principal working for a principal who has been hardened into enforcing the rules and running a "tight ship."

Now let us turn to some cases that have legal implications but also have extended ethical dimensions that might complicate making a proper decision.

Some Cases to Ponder

Case #1:
Michael is a third grade boy with special needs who is mainstreamed in a regular class. He is also from an abusive home in which his parents are rigid and use corporal punishment frequently. He is prone to verbally bullying boys who are smaller than him. Earlier this year, parents of two other boys in the class reported this to you, the principal, and demanded that

Michael be moved out of the school or they will sue. The district and school rules are clear; bullying is not tolerated. Today Michael has been sent to your office, charged by his teacher of verbal bullying. You know the phone will ring soon and it will be a parental call to remove Michael from the school. It is a painful decision, because you are a caring person.

1. What do you think you should do? Why would you do that?

2. Do you see a conflict between your sense of what is fair and just and your sense of compassion? Are there any ethical contradictions that come into play?

3. What are your legal duties in this case? Have you thought about the U.S. Supreme Court case, *Davis vs. Monroe*, that is very clear regarding the liability of a school administrator who knows of sexual harassment of one student to another but does nothing about it? Would the decision regarding sexual harassment transfer to bullying?

4. Is keeping Michael in the class, since he does have special needs, an option? The *Clyde vs. Puyallup* case tells us that a special needs child can be removed from a class if he is found to impede the learning of the other children in the class.

Case #2:
Marissa habitually uses vulgar language in the classroom. She has been told that this is not acceptable and that she will face some serious disciplinary sanctions if it does not stop. Marissa is currently living in a foster home with other older foster children placed by the court. The older foster children are "street smart" and regularly use this language in front of her. The principal is under pressure by her teacher to suspend Marissa. This will spare the teacher and Marissa's fellow students from having to hear vulgar language.

1. Once again we have a conflict between what is fair and just and what is the compassionate thing to do. What would you do and why?

2. Does the teacher have any rights to suspend Marissa? Would that be fair and just?

3. If you, as the principal, take the action of suspending Marissa, what steps must you take? Can following the law allow you to act ethically and compassionately as well?

————

Case #3:

You are aware that one of your teachers has been involved in petty theft for some time. It is always small amounts of money or supplies. The teacher is well liked by students, colleagues, and parents. The teacher is having some financial and marital problems at home which she has confided to you. Perhaps you should let it go. No one is complaining.

1. What are your ethical responsibilities in this case?

2. Are there legal as well as ethical matters involved?

3. If you discipline the teacher, you could risk alienating the staff and parents who would say you are being cold and insensitive. Does your sense of ethics allow this to be a consideration?

4. Are you incurring any professional liabilities regarding your own position if you do not act?

5. What will you do? Why will you do it? And how will you do it?

————

Case #4:

You are the principal of a middle school. One of your students, Marlene, comes to you and says that she has been harassed by three other girls in the school using a social media network site, including making hurtful remarks about her appearance, raising what she believes to be disturbing questions about her parents, and suggesting the world would be a better place without her around. You decide to talk with the girls who are making the alleged comments and after hearing their response, you decide to suspend them and recommend expulsion. They claim that never meant harm and were just engaging in gossip and fun, that their First Amendment rights are being violated, and that you have no authority in the matter anyway since it is their personal social media accounts that are in question, with no school computers being involved. To compound things, they are now suing you with the support of outside First Amendment advocacy groups.

1. Did you follow the law properly in disciplining the girls? What is the law regarding the facts of this case?

2. Do you see a conflict between your ethical responsibilities and your legal responsibilities in this matter?

3. Do the girls have a point regarding the fact that their statements were made on their personal social media pages and not at school?

4. Should the fact that you are being sued cause you to change your decision to discipline the girls?

Curriculum

In the introduction to his book, we noted—among other issues—some controversies that surround curriculum matters, most notably the pressures that rising test scores present. It is not uncommon to read of stories about district officials or principals engaging in possibly illegal and/or unethical practices that allow test scores to be raised. And that is not the only curriculum issue that confronts today's school leaders, although it is a compelling one. There are matters such as the pressure to change students' grades or to pressure teachers to do so since getting into a competitive college or university can be so difficult. Struggles over curriculum content is another matter that often is present in the news, whether it be the teaching of evolution, intelligent design, or the discussion of even the mention of gay sexual orientation in high school "cultural issues" classes.

Curriculum challenges can be daunting for the school leader because they often bring with them a conflict between one's own set of values and beliefs and those of some equally sincere and committed members of the community.

Some Cases to Ponder

Case #1:
You are the principal of Jefferson Elementary School that is under extreme pressure from the superintendent to raise test scores. In fact, you have been told that your job is on the line if scores do not improve this year, even though that is a most daunting task, with problems in the school and the community making the task even more than challenging. You have an opportunity to get an advance copy of the tests which will allow you to direct staff on how to raise achievement scores by teaching to the tests. Jefferson Elementary School serves a poor community and the students suffer low self-esteem. Raising scores will be good for the students. Your teachers need a morale boost. No one will ever know that you have this access. It is a win/win situation for everyone.

1. What are the ethical issues in this case? Are there ethical dilemmas you face or are things pretty straight forward?

2. What are you going to do? Why are you going to do that?

3. Since you alone have access to the tests and no one will ever know that, and since the school—not to say you

and your career—will benefit, does that make a difference and should that be taken into account?

4. Is "teaching to the tests" conceptually and topically, as opposed to lifting questions directly from advance copies of the test so that students can practice their answers before official tests are administered, ethically appropriate or not?

Case #2:
The son of the board president attends your school. He has been caught cheating on an examination. To issue a consequence will jeopardize his chances of getting into college. The student has a perfect record—high grades, no discipline referrals, and a history of significant service to the school and community. He is a prime candidate for admission to a prestigious college. The board president has always liked you and will expect you to help out in a situation like this. In addition, the teacher of the class in which the incident happened, likes both you and the board president and is willing not to make an issue of this publicly; rather, he has reported the matter to you in confidence and is awaiting your guidance on the matter.

1. Here you are asked to weigh personal loyalties against a school standard that is clear about cheating. What factors should you take into account?

2. If the board president tries to pressure you and even gets the teacher to join her in trying to persuade you to forget the whole matter, will that make a difference?

3. What will you do and why will you do it?

4. When you are confronted with an ethical dilemma such as this, how do you go about making your decision?

Case #3:

You are principal of Elvira Senior High School that is located in a middle/upper middle class area. The community is somewhat conservative politically and there are a number of churches in the area that have a strong influence in the community. These churches and other community organizations have been quite supportive of the school over the years. This year a new biology book is being introduced into the required curriculum. The book, which was approved following the district approved text-book adoption process, is in alignment with state curriculum standards. One chapter of the book deals with evolution and presents it as the explanation of the development of the human species. The chapter does not consider any other explanations of the origin of the human species. As the introduction of the text approaches for the next school year, some parents and then their pastors start a petition to withdraw the book or, at the least, to require that the theory of intelligent design that says the origin of the human species (and other species as well) is the result of divine intervention be included in the curriculum. You, personally because of your own religious beliefs, see the merit in that, but you also know that there is a history of case law that gives you guidance otherwise. After explaining why you cannot change the text, some of the pastors and community leaders say that they will encourage people not to support the school to the degree they had in the past. They feel very strongly about their beliefs and you understand their sincerity and even sympathize with them. Finally, you decide it is in the best interest of the school to withdraw the book, start a new textbook selection process, and assure that intelligent design is one of the approaches regarding the origin of the human species that is considered.

1. Was your decision, as described above, the right one to make? Why or why not?

2. Was it appropriate for you to factor in your own religious view in this matter, especially since it appeared to be consistent with the majority view of your school community?

3. Is your knowledge of case law, including the U.S. Supreme Court decision in *Edwards vs. Aguilar*, relevant?

4. Should the views of those who do not agree with "pulling" the book be taken into account?

5. In some states, only evolution can be taught in the curriculum. If you are living in one of those states, are you ethically as well as legally bound to exclude any other consideration of the origin of the human species from the curriculum?

~~~~

Case #4:

A new law, such as the ones that have been proposed in some state legislatures in recent years, has just been passed in your state that prohibits any mention or discussion of homosexuality in the classroom. Even if the curriculum does not explicitly mention homosexuality, any questions regarding being gay, lesbian, or transgender which might be raised by students in the classroom are to be ignored under penalty of law.

In the high school cultural issues class, marriage and other human relationships in society are studied. The teacher of the class comes to you, the principal, and informs you that there are some gay students in the class who have raised questions about human sexuality and non-heterosexual relationships. The teacher says she has ignored them, but because of the questions some members of the class have begun to taunt the gay students for having brought the subject up. The teacher also knows that some of the gay students are vulnerable regarding their sexual identity and that this situation could have unfortunate emotional and maybe even physical consequences for them. It is her belief that she must break the law and discuss these matters with all of the students openly and sympathetically. The teacher also informs you that she is gay.

1. Does this case present a conflict between the law and ethics? If so, why?

2. Is the fact that the teacher is gay relevant to the case?

3. What decision will you make? Will you support the teacher if she addresses the issue openly against the law?

4. Do you have any ethical responsibilities to the gay students in this matter? If so, what are they?

Communicating with Parents, Students, and Community Members

One of the greatest challenges of a school administrator is providing effective and skillful communications with parents, students, and the community members through various means on a variety of issues and matters. This component has become increasingly important with the advancement of technology (i.e., computer and Internet, smart phones, and social media with their easy access with their stakeholders). The importance of communicating properly is further accentuated with an aggressive press and their instant response to compete with social media and the Internet. These factors provide high stakes on the importance of skillful and effective communications because student, parent and community perceptions—along with the reputations of school districts, schools, and their administrators—are all are formed and reinforced based on the communications skills the administrators demonstrate.

Furthermore, a lack of communications from school administrators and/or their inability or unwillingness to communicate effectively and practice transparency with these stakeholders can create worse case scenarios with long lasting reputation and perception fall-out. Often, the most frequently asked questions regarding communications is who should communicate about what and through what means. Although volumes could be written about this subject alone, most school districts have school board policies and regulations on communications with the public, parents, students, and staff designating appropriate school district/school officials for communications and announcements.

Some Cases to Ponder

Case #1:
You are a new principal of an 800 student high school in a relatively isolated but tight-knit attractive rural community located in California's Sierra foothills. Teachers, administrators, and classified staff are known for long-term employment in the school district and eventually plan to stay in the community to raise their families because of the quality of life in this area. One evening after school, the head school custodian who has worked in the high school for the last five years, reports to you that he saw one of your veteran vice principals inappropriately touching a female high school student in his office. The next day, the district superintendent contacts you and reports that he heard the same report from a board member whose son attends the high school. He further reports that he is scheduling a special board meeting to report this incident, and that he is recommending paid administrative leave for this administrator, pending an investigation for possible criminal wrong-doing. He is asking you to schedule a meeting with the vice principal.

1. What role should you play in informing the vice principal of this incident?

2. Should you report this incident to local law enforcement?

3. How should you communicate this incident to parents, students, and staff?

4. Who should report this incident to the local press?

5. What involvement should you have in the investigation while the vice principal is on administrative leave with pay?

Case #2:

Dr. Confidence, superintendent of Center City School District, has just experienced a school board election in which two of his five members have just been elected to the Board of Trustees. These rookie board members have just attended their first board meeting. This board meeting included an executive session in which a discussion was held regarding the performance of a popular high school teacher, but no board action was taken. Under the Brown Act in California, personnel items are not to be shared with the public unless formal board action is taken. Unfortunately, Dr. Confidence has scheduled a new board member orientation regarding the Brown Act, working with the press, and many other issues essential for boardsmanship after this first board meeting because the new board members were unavailable to attend this orientation any earlier. These new board members, anxious to show their new power and "leadership skills," decided to leak executive session content to the local newspaper. Dr. Confidence just learned about this development after a reporter called him.

1. How should Dr. Confidence handle this situation?

2. If the newspaper editor decides to publish this story, how should Dr. Confidence communicate with parents, students, and staff?

3. How should the story be handled with the teacher who was the subject of the executive board session?

4. How should the two board members be dealt with to prevent a future recurrence of this incident?

Case #3:

The newspaper has just published the standardized test scores for all of the schools in the Exclusive Elementary School District, which dramatically impacts both the API and AYP. You are the principal of High Pressure Elementary School, which is located in an upper socio-economic area of the

District. The test scores of your School fell slightly in math in all grades, but more sharply in reading in the primary grades, and held steady in grades 4–6. This year's results mean that your school failed to make both the API and AYP for the first year and may become a Program Improvement (PI) school. By contrast, all of the other schools in the District made their API and AYP, although their student test scores were lower than High Pressure Elementary School. Parents will undoubtedly be concerned about this newspaper story.

1. How are you going to handle this newspaper story?

2. How will you communicate these test results to parents while maintaining the academic reputation of the school?

3. How will you report these results to the superintendent and school board?

4. What plan of academic improvement and implementation of this plan will you make for the school?

5. How will you communicate to and involve your teachers to provide AYP/API growth for next year?

Personnel Matters

There are many personnel matters that school leaders must deal with. Schools are human enterprises and they are a "people business." There is a vast body of leadership literature and many, if not most, programs that prepare school administrators have courses exclusively devoted to leadership. These courses examine a variety of leadership theories and strategies with many taken from fields other than education such as business and the military. We considered some of these theoretical approaches in an earlier chapter that reflected on philosophy and ethics, most notably when we considered Machiavelli and Hobbes.

There are different leadership styles that have an influence on the ethical behavior of school administrators and they have an impact on school personnel matters. Among those styles, all of which have their benefits, are—

Charismatic: leadership based on the force of personality and inspired loyalty of followers. This could lead to undue influence on the part of the school administrator.

Bureaucratic: leadership based on following the rules. This leader keeps order and does not entertain personal ethical dilemmas because the rules tell us what is right and what is wrong.

Transformational: leadership based in setting a vision that gets followers to buy into that vision and to identify with the leader's vision to noticeably change the organization for what is perceived by both the leader and followers to be better.

Situational: leadership based on the leader's understanding of where he or she believes a follower is regarding being able to act with or without strong direction. This approach can lead to a leader typecasting a follower as to the type of employee they are or can be.

What does this have to do with ethics and understanding personnel? Understanding leadership styles and relating them to personnel practices can help us understand how some leaders, perhaps without even thinking about it, can act not only according to their leadership style but also unethically (National University, 2011).

What follows are several style-based ethical scenarios. Let us look at them and consider the ethical issues involved.

Some Cases to Ponder

Case #1:

A Charismatic Leader: Dr. Strongly has just been hired as superintendent by the board of education to replace a long-time, more casual type administrator who has allowed things to drift. Dr. Strongly has a magnetic personality and is known for being a straight talker who will get people to do things right. Shortly after assuming his new position, he comes to the conclusion that his predecessor surrounded himself with likewise quiet, casual educators who had no spirit, many of whom had retired when he took over the superintendency. Dr. Strongly believes he must address all of the teachers and administrators in the district concerning his conclusions and name names to motivate the others to follow his bold new direction that will lead to re-invigorated success (National University, 2011).

1. Dr. Strongly has talent in his personality that allows him to motivate others. Should he openly display it even if it might make others uncomfortable?

2. Is it ethical for Dr. Strongly to name those he believes did have the right spirit in order to motivate the rest of the district staff?

3. Dr. Strongly is preparing to name the names in a public speech. Would it be less of an ethical concern if he decided not to do that but to name names in small groups or private conversations instead?

4. What ethical obligations does a school leader have regarding protecting the reputation of former employees, even those he or she believes have performed poorly and might even have hurt the institution?

Case #2:

A Bureaucratic Leader: Ms. Marmalade, who has been the district Director of Classified Personnel for years, receives a private memorandum from a school bus driver. She has heard in the break room between runs that the driver of the school bus for severely handicapped children—the ones who are incapable of communicating verbally—intimidates them with force and abusive language. It is impossible to talk with the children. Ms. Marmalade then talks to the students' teacher who cannot verify that there is any abuse, but she does observe that the children start to cry and do not want to go on the bus at the end of the day. This, she notes, was not the case when there was another driver last year. Ms. Marmalade has always been very careful to follow the procedures of the district and two of those procedures are that the accused employee must be informed so that he or she can protect his or her rights and a confidential investigation must be completed before any action is taken. Ms. Marmalade, even though she strongly suspects that the information in the memorandum may be true, will not depart from these procedures and she does not want to give the impression to any member of the staff that rules are there to be broken. The bus driver continues with her route for the severely handicapped students and the students continue to show anxiety at the end of the school day.

1. Is Ms. Marmalade correct in exhausting all processes and procedures before taking action?

2. What action, if any, do you think Ms. Marmalade will take and why should she take it?

3. Do you see any potential conflict between ethics and the law in this scenario? If so, what might those conflicts be?

4. Are there times when one is ethically bound to break the rules, even if it might set a bad precedent for the organization and might even threaten one's job?

Case #3:
A Transformational Leader: Mr. Vision, the new principal of the school, has determined that the culture of the school must be changed if student achievement is to improve and it is in sore need of improvement. After working with staff and parents to create a new vision, he is ready to implement it. There are some veteran teachers whose entire career has been at that school and who will be eligible to retire in a few years. They do not accept the conclusion that the culture needs to be changed. The plan is for them to be "let go" through carefully

planned cut-backs that affect their fields only. Mr. Vision is proud that he not only can transform the school, but also is sharp enough to figure out how to eliminate the resisting veteran teachers without having to deal with the union and the district contract (National University, 2011).

1. Is Mr. Vision acting ethically and selectively in proceeding forward and cleanly eliminating resistance to implementing a new vision (which is badly needed) if the students are to see their achievement improve?

2. Do the resisting veteran teachers have any ethical responsibilities that need to be addressed?

3. What should Mr. Vision do and why?

4. Are there two ethically valid imperatives competing here, and how does one resolve such a conflict if, indeed, one does exist?

Case #4:
A Situational Leader: Ms. Typology, who has been principal for some years and prides herself on knowing her teaching staff's levels of experience and behavior, is told that veteran teacher Mr. Battle, who is widely respected in the school has publicly berated an eighth grade boy such that he does not want to be in his class. She "knows" that is just the way Mr. Battle is and directs the boy to stay in the class and "take it like a man." Ms. Typology also is told that Ms. Novice has done the same thing in her eighth grade class. She thinks this might be a good learning experience for Ms. Novice and counsels her about her classroom management skills and also suggests that this may become an evaluation matter (National University, 2011).

1. Ms. Typology treats the two teachers differently regarding a similar situation. Is this ethical? Why or why not?

2. Is putting people into categories based upon reputation and/or experience a wise and ethical thing to do?

3.   Is having a different set of standards and/or expecta-
     tions for different members of one's staff for the same
     kinds of situations appropriate? Can it be an effective
     and ethical leadership behavior?

4.   How would you recommend that Ms. Typology handle
     this situation?

~

Case #5:

The Job Opening: Your school has an administrative opening.
There is an established set of district procedures for the selection of a candidate. You, as the principal, convene the interview
team and begin the process. What your colleagues on the team
do not know is that the superintendent has told you whom he
wants selected and that it is your job to see that it happens.
Your job is to steer the selection process through debriefing
discussions, etc., to reach the desired outcome. The interview
process is for show.

1.   Should you confront the superintendent and tell him
     that you cannot do this, or is it best that you follow di-
     rections since it is—as the superintendent reminds
     you—for the good of the district?

2.   How would you, personally, handle this request? If you
     were a close friend of the superintendent and you know
     he will be loyal to you, does that make a difference?

3.   Do you have an ethical obligation to your colleagues on
     the interview team to let them know what the superin-
     tendent's agenda is and to allow them to decline serving
     on the selection committee if that is their choice?

4.   Do you have any ethical obligations to the candidates
     who are not to be selected? If so, what are those
     obligations?

~

Athletics

There is no question that high school and collegiate competitive sports generate more interest, publicity, and often controversy than almost any other issue in schools or colleges. Featured stories include athletic super-stars, outstanding teams, coaches being hired or fired, or illegal/unethical player recruiting practices. Often, the reputation of the school is made more from its success on the football field, basketball court, baseball diamond, or track field than from student academic achievement.

With the ultimate goal of winning games, becoming league champions, winning Bowl Championship Series (BCS), and generating gate and television revenue, large college football coaches are paid incredible salaries and bonuses ranging from $350,000 per year up to $6 million per year (Urban Meyer, Ohio State University), $5.1 million per year (Mack Brown, University of Texas), etc., as long as they win games (*USA Today*, 2011). Furthermore, wealthy donors such as billionaire T. Boone Pickens and BP Capital Executive contributed millions to the Oklahoma State University Cowboys. Phil Knight (Nike Co-Founder and Chairman) contributed millions to the University of Oregon Ducks to supplement coaches' salaries and pay for the development of state of the art athletic facilities (i.e., football stadiums, indoor practice arenas, and basketball pavilions, etc.) that would be unaffordable by the local community (Rosenburg, 2011) and (Weiberg, 2011).

While high school athletic coaches' compensation does not compare with college football coaches' salaries, in some states (i.e., Texas), a high school football coach will average $114,000/year, often twice as much as he would make as a classroom teacher.

However, there is often a dark, unethical side to the spotlight of high revenues for athletic programs, college football, stratospheric coaches' salaries, full athletic scholarships for athletes including all paid expenses, and glaring publicity for athletic superstars. In the quest for colleges and universities to have winning teams and league championships, questionable, unethical, and often-illegal player recruiting practices happen with or without university or coaches' knowledge. Such practices precipitate endless League and/or National Collegiate Athletic Association (NCAA) investigations, often resulting in severe penalties for the entire sport's season for those having knowledge of these unethical practices. Private recruiters are hired and generously paid, in violation of NCAA rules and regulations, to personally contact and recruit athletic superstars out of high schools and community colleges.

At the high school level, high school state interscholastic federations conduct equivalent investigations and also impose penalties in an effort to police and enforce ethical high school athletic programs. Often, high school athletes are provided housing in a high school attendance area, despite living elsewhere with their parents, making them "eligible" to play a major team sport at a high school with a prestigious championship team. The practices at some of these offending schools have created an environment of an occasional student superathlete getting into trouble with the law for drunk driving, speeding violations, possession of drugs, burglaries, and thefts, etc. All of these practices and highly publicized incidents are unethical and serve to tarnish the image of a college and its athletic program, along with the athlete star role model image to millions of young people.

Some Cases to Ponder

Case #1:
You are the high school principal of a large high school in an urban school district in a lower socio-economic area. The basketball team at your school is currently locked in a two-way tie for first place and is scheduled to play a rival basketball team across town next Friday evening. The local media, students, and fan base are really excited about this game. Unexpectedly, your athletic director, basketball coach, and athletic booster club president telephone you requesting an immediate meeting with you. You meet with them and hear about the center's current academic problem—he has received an unsatisfactory

progress report in his English class. He is performing satisfactorily in all of his other classes. They are asking you to talk with the English teacher to see if anything can be done about reversing this problem so he can play that all-important game this coming Friday night. They are deeply concerned that the team may not win without his playing in that game. State interscholastic regulations prohibit academically ineligible athletes from playing. However, you are concerned that the booster club, fan base, students, and community will not understand denying this star center from playing because of a correctable academic problem.

1. Should you contact the English teacher to see what can be done about this student?

2. What should you do if the English teacher tells you that the earliest the student can resume satisfactory progress in his class is not until after Friday's football game?

3. Should you overrule the English teacher with the understanding that the center can restore his satisfactory progress before the end of the grading period?

4. What will you say to the football coach, athletic director, and booster club president?

~~~~~~

Case #2:
You are the high school principal of Flatline High School, a small rural high school in the center of California. Your school's football team is locked into a first place tie with Tomatoland High School, an arch rival high school. This has been the case between the two football teams for several years in a row. The league championship game between these two high schools is scheduled for next Friday at Tomatoland's football field and stadium. According to California Interscholastic Federation (CIF), the high school competitive athletic rules and

enforcement agency, the home team wears dark colored uniforms and the visiting team wears light colored uniforms. You and your wife have decided to attend what promises to be an exciting football game. Your superintendent and some members of your district school board also decide to attend. While sitting in the Tomatoland High School's stadium in the visitor section, the home team is cheered by approximately 2,500 students and fans making their entry wearing their dark uniforms. To your complete surprise, Flatline High School's football team now makes its entry onto the field also wearing their home team dark uniforms. Under the lights, both teams with dark uniforms are very difficult to distinguish. The home team fans have quickly picked up on this problem with a chorus of boos and other uncomplimentary comments. How can this football game proceed when both teams are wearing dark uniforms, making it difficult for players to distinguish teams? You know what the California Interscholastic rules are regarding uniforms.

1. As the principal of the visiting team, what will do about this situation? Will you allow the game to continue given the excitement and enthusiasm of the fans?

2. Will you allow the game to proceed under these rule violations?

3. Who are the first stakeholders you should talk with? What will you say to them?

4. What will you tell California Interscholastic Federation? Your superintendent?

5. What action will you take with your athletic director and football coach?

Case #3:
You are a high school assistant principal in charge of student behavior and student activities including athletics at Mediocre High school, which is located in a middle class neighborhood

that places a high value on competitive athletics. The school attendance secretary walks into your office and announces that several student football athletes have recently enrolled, transferring from other high schools across town, and wanting to play football. Perceiving something unusual, you decide to investigate by talking to one or more of the new students. They report to you that each student has been given several hundred dollars to enroll at Mediocre High School, and that they're living with members in the community within the school attendance boundaries. Upon further inquiry from the community members boarding these students, they report being paid from a "source" for room and board expenses. Later, the assistant principal learned from the athletic director, who was asked not to divulge the sources, said the money came from the school booster club. This practice is strictly against California Interscholastic Federation regulations.

1. What will you do to investigate and stop this unethical practice?

2. Will you inform the principal and perhaps the superintendent?

3. How will you discipline the athletic director for accepting these funds?

4. How will you inform the California Interscholastic Federation?

5. How will you handle the booster club to stop this practice while maintaining good relations with them?

Sex, Politics, and Religion

Hardly a day goes by when there is not a story somewhere in the media about a teacher or an administrator acting inappropriately in the school setting, often with a student. In many ways, the story is sensationalized and the reputations not only of the accused, but also of the other teachers and administrators in the school are severely called into question. It is important to be aware not only of the laws but also of one's ethical responsibilities when confronted with such an issue.

Engaging in politics can be a controversial venture and for school administrators it can also be a career ending venture. Not only are there legal requirements to be aware of but there are also ethical responsibilities to consider. This refers not just to external political matters and freedom of expression, but also the internal political dynamics that govern a school and/or district.

And as we have observed in earlier chapters, one's personal religious values are a fundamental part of one's ethical core. But, as we also have noted, these values and those of community members can create a conflict for us as we try to make sound ethical and legal judgments. Striking a balance between our personal values and those that are different can create ethical problems for us as we make significant leadership decisions. It is important that we are comfortable and confident in striking that balance.

Some Cases to Ponder

Case #1:

You are the principal of XYZ High School. It has been reported to you by some students that one of your teachers, Ms. Charm, a 38-year-old English teacher who is also married and the mother of two middle school age children, has been having an affair with one of her 18-year-old male students who is in her honors course. He is from an impoverished home and has been essentially forced out of his home by his parents because of their disintegrating family situation. You decide to discuss this matter with Ms. Charm because it does disturb you that the report might be true. Ms. Charm denies that anything inappropriate has taken place; however, she does confirm that she took him into her house after her husband left her because of their marital problems. Further, she tells you that after the student graduates, it is her hope that they will marry and that she will be able to support him in his future academic career.

1. Do you have any legal obligations to act in this situation? Do you have any ethical obligations to act even if you do not have any legal obligations because of the student's age?

2. Do you have any legal responsibilities regarding the student? Are there any court cases that might be relevant?

3. Do you have any ethical responsibilities regarding the student's disintegrating family situation, especially his being forced to leave his home?

4. Do you have any ethical responsibilities regarding the teacher's children and what might be happening at present? Is her future hope regarding marriage a matter you should be concerned about?

5. What will you do in this situation? How do you know it is the right thing to do?

Case #2:

You are the principal of Homer Elementary School, which is in an upper middle class area with parents who are high achieving and have high aspirations for their children. One of the parents in your school is the local state assembly person for the area. She has been most supportive in getting state technology grants for the school through her influence with a certain member of the state department of education. This year she faces a difficult re-election campaign and asks you to help her by hosting a fund-raiser at the school and by openly encouraging other parents to support her campaign because their support and your support will support the schools. Also, the superintendent is her close friend and she, too, encourages you to enter the political arena with your support. To compound the matter, while you are grateful for all of the help she has given to the school over the years, you are not a supporter of her political party. This is a matter you discreetly avoid talking about and you generally support a philosophy on other issues that are different from those she espouses.

1. Here you may have an ethical conflict between promoting the good of the school and its students and your lack of comfort in doing what you are being asked to do. What priority should come first?

2. What does your sense of ethics say you should do?

3. Are there any legal issues involved in this scenario?

4. What will you do, realizing that you have a lot of pressure on you, including pressure from the superintendent?

5. Should partisan politics and effective school leadership ever mix?

Case #3:
It is holiday time and you are the principal of your community's only middle school. Every year the school has sponsored a Christmas pageant, which was somewhat religious in orientation, reflecting the prevailing sentiment of the majority of the parents. This also reflects your sentiments as well. The local churches have provided many resources to make this annual event a success and most of the students always look forward to participating in the singing, orchestral performances, and Biblical re-enactments of the events celebrated by the season. This year, however, some parents of newly arrived Islamic students approach you and inform you that they do not want to have their children participate in the pageant and that further, they believe it is inappropriate for the pageant to be sponsored by the school at all. You take this concern to your parent advisory group (which does not include the Islamic parents) and to the local clergy association. They say that a minority of parents should not have a right to stop this event which is favored by

the majority. Instead, they recommend that the Islamic students be excused from any participation in the event itself and
from any rehearsals conducted during school time as well. They
also remind you of your own religious connections to the community and that to "stray" would show ineffective leadership on
your part. You know the law regarding this issue, but you also
know that it has been conveniently avoided over the years
because there never was an objection before.

1.   What does the law say regarding this case? What court
     cases are relevant?

2.   In addition to your legal responsibilities, do you have
     any ethical responsibilities to address the matter? What
     are those responsibilities and what are they based on?

3.   You realize that changing the yearly holiday pageant
     will bring some discomfort to the Islamic students from
     the majority of students who will taunt them and
     maybe even isolate them. Ethically, can you allow this
     to happen, or is this just the consequence they will have
     to suffer for being the center of an unpopular, contro-
     versial community matter?

4.   Making any changes will, undoubtedly, hurt your
     standing in the school community. Should this make a
     difference?

5.   What will you do and why will you do it?

References

Hartman, W. T., & Stefkovich, J. A. (2005). Ethics for school business officials (pp. 3–7). Roman and Littlefield.

National University Online Course Shell, EDA 651, Lecture 2B.

"Nike's Phil Knight has branded Oregon into national power." Michael Rosenburg: Inside football. Retrieved from SI.com. (2011, January 11).

Daniel, S. "Paso Robles police chief gets $230K for damage to reputation after sex-harassment claim." San Luis Obispo Tribune. (2012, March 22).

Weiberg, S. (2011, January 28). "Pickens understands UConn donor's anger." *USA Today*.

"USA TODAY college football coach salary database, 2006–2011." Retrieved from USA today.com

References

(text illegible)

Chapter 7

Some Concluding Thoughts

Ethics is a complex subject. On the one hand, it is the study and perhaps the reaffirmation of core values one has through their religion, their culture, and as some philosophers suggest, from their very nature of being human. On the other hand, ethics is not a constant, but an evolving approach to decision making that must be viewed from the context in which decisions are made, changing culture values, and even time and place.

Only recently, for example, we have seen a profound change in how many people view the issue of gay marriage. For many people, holding steadfast to traditional and religious values, the proper response to this issue was determined thousands of years ago by imperatives that do not need or allow for re-thinking. But there is also another side to the issue. This side acknowledges that we know much more about human sexuality now than we did even generations ago. We also personally know or know of some same-sex couples who are in loving and committed relationships and rearing children. For others, this has become an issue of human rights, a major component in setting one's ethical compass. Even a President of the United States was moved to affirm his acceptance and support of gay marriage in an uncertain political environment. Good people, as we see, can disagree profoundly, ethically, and morally on an issue that has significant consequences on how we accept or reject members of our society and the kinds of behavior we will or will not embrace.

Setting Our Ethical Compass as School Leaders

Throughout this book we have used the term "ethical compass." Is there such a thing? That is hard to say and defining that term is as complex as the subject of ethics itself. The term "ethical compass" is really a metaphor for setting the direction we, both as individuals and as school leaders, must follow as we are faced with the often difficult and consequential decisions that we must make. And while it might be easier to define how we as individuals will act in making personal decisions, that is not always the case when we make decisions affecting those who do not share our beliefs or have a very different set of settings for their personal ethical compasses. Making ethical decisions as a school leader is a demanding social and personal responsibility that can transcend our own values.

In Chapter 1, we raised the question of why we study ethics. There can be little doubt that ethics has become a subject of great concern not only in business (which has had its share of scandals), but also to problems in the schools that are equally troubling and challenging to school leaders. Using the words of Warren Bennis, we need to understand the distinction between managers and leaders, a distinction in which managers do things right and leaders do the right thing. While that is an interesting play on words, it is a significant one. The ethical school leader is a leader who does the right thing. Determining what the "right thing" is demands that we call upon all of our values—those from our own culture, religious beliefs, and those we attain through our study of philosophy and practice.

In Chapter 2, we examined the writings of a number of significant ethical/moral philosophers from the Western tradition who have helped define how we respond to different moral problems. It is not our intent as authors to endorse any one of these approaches to ethical thinking, but it is our hope that these philosophers have shed some light on how future school leaders might arrive at the place where they can fall back upon a rationale that explains why they have the ethical compass they have. Do we believe in absolute, transcendent virtue, and morality as Plato teaches or do we see ethics to be a study of the habit of virtue and the mean of action as Aristotle suggests? Is Machiavelli correct when he tells us that it is better for a leader to be feared than to be loved and that all people are fickle and devoted to their self-interest? Is Hobbes correct when he writes that without strong and directive leadership the state—and by extension the schools we shall lead—will descend to a state of nature where "life is short, nasty, and brutish"? From a different perspective, there is Kant's categorical imperative that tells us, "Always act so that you can will the maximum or determining principle of your action to become universal law; act so that you can will that everybody shall follow the principle of your action." Will that view be the one that helps us set our ethical compass? And we must not forget John Rawls who calls our attention to the need to focus on justice and our social responsibility to be aware of how our ethical decisions affect others and whether or not they advance the common good. Also, it is important that we consider Kohlberg who concludes that people can develop a sense of ethics over time and that there are, in fact, developmental stages we go through as we mature—if we do—ethically.

In Chapter 3, we drew distinctions between codes of ethics, standards, and principles, linking them as rough measures of acceptable performance. We gave example codes of ethics and bills of rights from various well-known professional organizations. While we stated that standards and principals are supposed to be neutral for race, gender, class, religion, ethnicity, and sexual orientation, in reality they are not. Instead, they often carry a hidden agenda that reflects religious or political sources, rendering them as value judgments.

We also stated that standards are supposed to give the public a sense of confidence that professional educators are highly competent in discharging their duties. The reality is that standards assure only minimal performance, conformity, and accountability; they may, in fact, discourage the high-quality leadership, innovation, and creativity to move an organization to higher levels.

We gave particular emphasis to Standard 5, one of the ISLLC (Interstate School Leaders Licensure Consortium) Standards called *Understanding Rights and Common Good,* implying the impact of ethical decisions on the total school community (i.e., students, parents, staff, and community stakeholders and the impact of decision making on individual stakeholder rights). As we noted, a difficult challenge for the school leader is to determine what should be the correct emphasis a leader should give to his or her decision. At the same time, regarding Standard 5, we also observed that leaders are obligated to accept responsibility for their decision making. They cannot blame high-level administrators or the school board for their site decisions. Most importantly, school leaders must have a caring attitude and sensitivity for individual rights. They must focus on the total school community and make their school the best it can be.

In Chapter 4, diversity and ethical decision making in the schools were examined with the observation that making ethical decisions is a complex matter. An aspiring educational leader needs to develop his or her own moral compass, since there is no single or easy approach to decision making. This complexity compels a leader to understand that moral compass when confronted with not only diversity in values, but also how those values affect our thinking regarding cultures, race, equity, religion, leadership and power, gender, and attitudes toward the disabled—to name but a few variables.

In Chapter 4, we also contended that ethical issues of cultural pluralism emerge when the practices and policies of educators reflect the culture, mores, and needs of the dominant class (in the case of school administration, white and middle-class males), which are often in opposition to the culture and interests of non-dominant groups. The issue is not whether individuals and groups are treated similarly or differently, but rather whether treatment results in inequitable effects. Considerable research confirms that consciously or sub-consciously, decisions from the dominant class may not favor the non-dominant class and tend to keep them in their place.

In Chapter 5, we examined school leadership and ethics from a woman's perspective. Of particular interest was the author's discussion comparing male and female leadership ethics. Dr. Salice argued that in the past there has been a cadre of male leaders who have committed ethical violations against female followers and then protected themselves by forming an informal "club" that does nothing to censure or curtail such actions. Women leaders have been too small in numbers to form a similar club to protect themselves from these actions or to seek solutions to these ethical challenges. It may be, in fact, that women may have a stronger ethical compass, precluding them from joining the "club." Instead, as Dr. Salice observed, women must act independently, often with courage, compassion, and commitment to do the "right thing." The problem, though, is that women must learn to "fit in" the male leadership model to survive, but lack the "gravitas" to be taken seriously when making important decisions.

Dr. Salice cited references that men are more likely to consider moral issues in terms of justice, rules, and individual rights. Women, on the other hand, tend to consider such issues in terms of relationship, caring, and compassion. When confronted with a moral conflict, the research validates the argument that women look beyond the issue of justice and rules, and attempt to see a bigger picture that involves feelings, attitudes, perceptions, and even interpretations. Viewing the bigger picture, women are more sensitive to moral issues that have an effect on their decisions and their impact on their school and community. The chapter ends with the conclusion that a school leader's ethical decision making process should not be determined by gender stereotypes.

Chapter 6 focused on the application of what was examined throughout the book, concentrating on ethical decision making challenges school leaders face in several different areas. These areas include business and school finance, school law, curriculum, parent, student and community member communications, and difficult personnel matters: implementation of collective bargaining contracts, athletics, and last but not least, the most controversial topics of sex, politics, and religion. We approached each of these topics with a brief introduction of each topic and then followed with the presentation of some case studies to analyze. The case studies are based upon actual situations experienced by the authors of this book or situations inspired by cases reported by the news media.

In the end, however, it is not what we have read or discussed that will be most important. Rather, it is who we are or who we have become—what we believe, why we believe it, and how we shall act upon those beliefs. As a final activity in our consideration of Ethics for Today's School Leaders: Setting Our Ethical Compass, we, as authors, ask you to draw a picture of your own personal, ethical compass. Make a circle with three parts that states (in three or four bullet points for each part) the following: your ethical beliefs as an individual, your ethical beliefs as a school leader, and your code for taking ethical action. Let what we have considered in this text be your guide and keep this compass for your future reference.

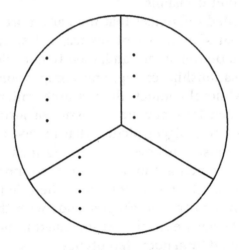

As we have stated repeatedly, ethics is a complex subject. But in many ways, it need not be. We hope that this text has helped you think through your own ethical development and that you share—not only in words but also, and more importantly, in action—your ethical compass with all whom you encounter in your career as a school leader.